POLICING INNOCENCE

POLICING INNOCENCE

Is your child really safe?

Rebecca Andrews

Authentic

MILTON KEYNES ● COLORADO SPRINGS ● HYDERABAD

14 13 12 11 10 09 08   8 7 6 5 4 3 2 1

First published 2008 by Authentic Media
9 Holdom Avenue, Bletchley, Milton Keynes, MK1 1QR, UK
1820 Jet Stream Drive, Colorado Springs, CO 80921, USA
OM Authentic Media, Medchal Road, Jeedimetla Village,
Secunderabad 500 055, A.P., India
www.authenticmedia.co.uk

Authentic Media is a division of IBS-STL U.K., a company limited by guarantee, with its Registered Office at Kingstown Broadway, Carlisle, Cumbria
CA3 0HA. Registered in England & Wales No. 1216232. Registered charity
270162

British Library Cataloguing in Publication Data
A catalogue record for this book is available from the British Library

ISBN-13: 978-1-86024-626-5

Names have been changed to protect identities.

Cover Design by Richard Wood Photography
Print Management by Adare Carwin
Printed in Great Britain by J.H. Haynes & Co., Sparkford

Contents

Acknowledgements

I need to say thank you to some very special people who have made this book happen. Firstly, my family – your faithful love and patient support is beyond words. You are all simply the best, the very best. Thank you, Richard, for your unwavering belief in me as a writer – you are much of the reason I didn't give up long ago. To my close colleagues in the Paedophile Unit – you've been brilliant to me. Your input on a personal and professional level is deeply valued; if only coppers like you grew on trees! And thank you to Malcolm — you caught hold of the spirit of this book from the very beginning. Thank you for your foresight and courage. Speaking of courage – what a great editor I was given! You made a scary process very positive Sheila. I am so grateful to you. To Richard Wood Photography – thank you for your skill and professionalism. Finally, *blessed be the name of the Lord*. Jesus, you are my way, my truth and my life. I cannot imagine contemplating a day without you and am eternally grateful that I don't have to.

Rebecca Andrews

Introduction

Paedophiles . . . perverts . . . nonces . . . kiddy-fiddlers
. . . child-molesters . . . sex offenders . . . We all think we
know what we mean when we use those words. But do
we *really* know what we mean?

Too many people are ignorant about how paedophiles
operate with remarkable precision and patience as they
abuse children. None of us can afford to be unaware of
how cunningly they identify their targets, devise their
strategies, lay their groundwork, and then move in for
the kill. They are predators of the most manipulative
nature, operating under the very noses of the people
they most want to avoid. That is part of their skill: to be
abusing a child among the adults whose role it is to protect that little one from abuse.

Wild animals drag their prey away from the herd to
destroy it – paedophiles leave theirs in the place of safety
where they find them. They then create clever and imagi-
native ways of destroying the child in their own sur-
roundings, without anyone noticing. Would you spot this
happening where you are? And how do the enforcement
agencies cope with paedophiles?

The rise and rise of the Internet has been a pervert's
haven, creating a whole new world in which to hunt

1

children – again right amid the family home and always at the risk of various enforcement agencies tracking their activities.

This book is about exposing paedophiles, and the devious webs they weave to ensnare and destroy children . . . yours, mine, anybody's.

Let me set out my stall. I am a committed Christian, a wife, a mum – and a police officer. I have served professionally in the area of child protection for a number of years: convicting offenders, interviewing children and working in the Internet world of indecent images of children. Domestically, my husband and I are raising our two beautiful daughters whom we love more than our own lives. That is the standpoint from which I write this book – as a law enforcer and protector of children both inside and outside my front door. I have not a jot of geniality towards people who abuse children and know very little about the analysis of their behaviour in clinical terms. What I do know a lot about is the reality of their offences, how abusers conduct themselves to perpetrate their crimes and, therefore, how everyone else can take practical and effective measures to protect the innocent from harm.

I recognize that this is not a pleasant subject to talk about – hey, even paedophiles recognize that! Some months ago a colleague and I were travelling to a police station with an offender who had just been arrested on suspicion of possessing indecent images of children, as part of an early morning raid. When we had arrived at his address there were a few initial clues as to his 'tendencies': despite the fact that it was 6.30 in the morning, this single middle-aged man had pornography on his computer and Barbie on the telly, both playing at the same time. The place was a mess and so was he, especially when he donned a long black coat that reached beyond his ankles, making him look like the Grim Reaper. During the journey to the police station he attempted to discuss the allegations with me in the car, but this is a major legal no-no, and I told him I couldn't talk to him about the offence until we were in a formal tape-recorded interview. He dejectedly replied, 'I don't blame you. I wouldn't want to talk to a paedophile either.'

Revolting as this subject is, it is also imperative that society does not bury the issues surrounding child sex offenders in an attempt to escape their vulgarity. Paedophiles are not going to go away, so we must live with them among us, educate ourselves about how to defend our children and shut down all efforts made to defile them. We need to know as much about the subject as the offenders do; if you are fighting a highly skilled enemy it is utter folly to remain as uninformed as they are informed. You are immediately on the losing side – and the consequences of that are grim; fatal sometimes. Sticking your head in the sand always obscures your vision and leaves you – your children in this case – very vulnerable indeed. This book is about educating and not scaremongering, but it is not for the faint-hearted. Child abuse never is.

When our children were born we bought a number of books about child health, designed to educate us and keep them healthy. The books tend to illustrate worst case scenarios to make their points and they genuinely leave us questioning the possibility of meningitis every time one of the girls has a temperature. The likelihood of them contracting such a disease is slight – most temperatures signify something far less worrying – but the possibility is so terrible we look for the symptoms and act accordingly. This book is the child protection equivalent of all those health books; it is designed to keep your children safe. The factors relating to child protection are often explored through worst case scenarios and if you identify any of the factors in your own household it may highlight a concern you need to address but it doesn't automatically diagnose sexual abuse. I would ask that you read the book in the same way as you would health manuals: learn the symptoms and guard against them, but remember that while temperatures always need addressing they don't always mean meningitis.

Sexually abusing children is not something that paedophiles 'do'. It is something they 'are' – in much the same way, I believe, as your sexual orientation is who you are, not what you sometimes feel like doing. I am a heterosexual female – it is who I am. I couldn't be homosexual if I tried, because that's not who I am. Oh, I can acknowledge a pretty woman with a body to die for – usually begrudgingly – but she doesn't touch my hormones. I'm too busy comparing my rather thin legs and post-birth tummy to her lines of perfection and hoping she's pulling in her stomach so tightly it hurts. Her beauty breeds anything but attraction in me. But show me a picture of raw and rugged masculinity, and it's a different matter.

Paedophiles are innately attracted to children. It's a sickening disturbance that originates at the core of their personality; you can't stop it, you can't change it and neither can they. That's why they are so dangerous – because they are so driven. As a committed Christian I do believe that the power of Jesus Christ can change anyone but for that to happen they must co-operate with the working of his power in their life. Other than Christ, paedophiles can, at the very best, only be controlled and managed, but I don't think we or they can ever make the drive to abuse children go away. In my years of working with paedophiles, as a British police officer, I have never met a paedophile who has truly wanted to stop abusing children. Far from it – instead, the desire to abuse over-takes their life and defines their existence to the point that they will stop at nothing to ensure their perversions are satiated. But that's another thing – I've never met a paedophile who has been satiated. The meeting of one urge just seems to breed new ones that require his atten-tion. So, folks, our country is inhabited with literally thousands of perverts, all of whom are powerfully driv-en to abuse children, and the more they do so, the more they want to. We cannot afford to remain in the dark about how they go about it.

Child abuse has been prevalent throughout history as well as within our present-day society; in essence it will always be with us. However, I do believe a good propor-tion of the crimes committed are preventable if we turn our minds to the issues involved in shielding children and creating a watertight environment for them. If the public knew what to look out for in an offender lining up a child for abuse, and the enforcement agencies knew how to adequately control abusers through the justice system, there would be less child abuse committed among us.

Many of the kids depicted in the filth on the Internet are living in impoverished countries where anything goes for a few dollars, including parents selling their chil-dren to paedophiles in order to survive. These massive issues of poverty are not for discussion here – though next time you hear the phrase 'Make Poverty History' I implore you to add to your thinking that in doing so we make some child abuse history too. But if child abuse was solely the result of poverty, we would not have such an epidemic of it in boarding schools that are full of wealthy children, and yet have long been favoured estab-lishments in which to operate as a paedophile.

I am not going to address the issue of how poverty versus wealth impacts on the prevalence of abuse in this book, but I am going to explore how abusers abuse, and how they groom a child ready for abuse – and don't forget that that means grooming the adults around the child not to notice the abuse, just as much as it means grooming the child to suffer it. The protective circle must be as manipulated as the target, otherwise the offences cannot succeed. I am going to explore the gruesome reality of the Internet for parents and children alike and how this monster is policed, along with drawing on my own experiences as a police officer, parent and committed Christian. Churches are known targets for paedophiles, and I have dedicated a section of this book to exploring all aspects of that tragic reality – some taken from my own difficult experiences as child protection co-ordinator at a church I used to attend.

Throughout the book you will see that I draw heavily on real cases I have dealt with, to illustrate what I am saying. Nothing explains real life better than real life, and there seems little point in burbling on at you about matters that a true-life case can paint for you with much more interest. Some stories will make you smile, but most will make you recoil in horror and wonder why you pay your taxes. The chapter about police and courts is not comfortable reading – and I'm a cog in its wheel. The Criminal Justice System may not appear too 'just' to you by the end of this book, which is another reason why we all need to defend ourselves against paedophiles as best we can because, in my opinion, the system offers little protection of its own. And then there's one of the ultimate taboos amid this world of taboos – women who sexually abuse children. By the time you put this book down you may be feeling a bit queasy, but you'll know more about how to protect your child, which doesn't seem like a bad deal to me.

Our justice system is supposed to adhere to the principle that the protection of children is paramount above all other factors. Sadly, this declaration has become an empty set of words when it should be the heartbeat that pumps the lifeblood into all our policies, guidelines and decisions. This book is about what *you* can do; if the Powers-That-Be knew what to do with paedophiles and had the resolve to do it, this book wouldn't have been written.

Put it his way: if paedophilia was a contagious disease affecting our children, the government would have spent millions of pounds on comprehensive vaccination programmes, free information leaflets in the mail, specialist hospital wards, school nurses, and compensation systems with a bottomless pit of cash. But paedophiles are harming our children to a greater extent in this country than any childhood disease I know, and many adults remain unaware of the complexities involved.

To be fair, perverts are not always easy to spot; if only they wore a sandwich board declaring 'I abuse children, avoid me like the plague' (I'd rather get the plague). But sadly they often deliberately appear far nicer than everyone else, which is how they infiltrate a child's circle to destroy them: a façade of decency is fundamental to their success. And they come in all sorts of shapes and sizes. There are no stereotypes, no vocations, no races more or less likely to have perverts among them. However, picture the scene . . .

He's a male in his mid-sixties and has a bald head, save for a long flop of stubborn hair strands that travel sideways over his bald patch. The strands move as a block together, never as individual wisps, and he often lifts them back into place when they tumble as one past his ear. He always wears a dirty anorak, come rain or shine, and it emits a pungent whiff, largely because it is held in place more by the strength of his body odour than the strength of the buttons – of which there are two missing. His trousers don't quite reach his ankles as they fight a losing battle to cling to his paunch, and his socks are a dirty yellow colour. He hangs around parks a lot, and has a hole in his anorak pocket for convenience because he occasionally feels compelled to flash his manhood at females who walk his way. His smarmy smile is so slippery you could ski down it and, while his left hand is available for pocket action at all times, his right hand clasps a lukewarm bottle of cheap cider – well free actually because he nicked it.

If this caricature is what you envisage when you hear the word 'paedophile', then I urge you to think again. Such an individual is probably content playing his pathetic flashing game and not half as scary as the unseen menace encroaching on a child's life without anyone noticing. 'Dirty Ernie' from the park exposes himself in more ways than one, because now we all know he's a pervert. The secret's out! (So to speak.) It's the offender who conceals his activities as obsessively as he perpetuates them that we should be worrying about. This book wants to expose him too.

(A quick note on the offence of 'flashing': In my experience, flashing is an entirely male undertaking, and it has always struck me as incredibly sad. However, it breeds immense fear in women who are usually taken by surprise and always thinking beyond the exposed item to what the flasher may be intending to do with it next. The power of flashing doesn't so much lie in the exposure itself, as in the terror of more serious offences to come. It is a paradox to me – strangely comical and potentially lethal at the same time.

A few years ago I attended the home address of an elderly woman who had been flashed at by a Dirty Ernie while she was walking her dog in the park. It was the usual story that the offender was waiting among a small clump of trees in the middle of an otherwise open stretch of ground and, as the elderly lady walked nearby, he whisked open his coat to reveal that he had nothing on underneath. (You've never got a stun-gun with you when you need it, have you?) Anyway, I settled down to take this woman's statement and offer the appropriate sympathy, reassurance and advice when she continued, 'And officer, I tell you, dear, he had more than most under that coat of his. He was quite a sight, I tell you. Why, I went back this morning to see if he was still there.' I'm not often speechless, but I did struggle for a suitable reply on that occasion!)

There are many varieties of child sex offenders, driven by a singular impulse that manifests itself in a myriad of ways. As well as the offender who commits the actual abuse himself is the growing army of offenders who are gratified to watch other people committing the abuse via the Internet and its wealth of indecent images depicting children, more commonly known as *child pornography*.

Do not underestimate child pornography.

One of the most recent videos I saw was a four-minute clip in which an adult male was attempting to rape a three-year-old girl. A second adult – this time a female – was holding a camcorder to record the event, and the footage began with the little girl lying naked on her back at the end of a bed while he stood on the floor next to her. He was also naked. He dragged her tiny body towards his full grown one and attempted to penetrate her genitals with his own. Remember the bit about her being tiny and him being full grown? It was barely physically possible, exacerbated by her extreme distress. He became increasingly angry when he was unable to achieve his intentions, so in frustration he grabbed her tiny ankles, picked her up off the bed, flipped her over and slapped her back down again, this time lying on her tummy. It reminded me of the way a fishmonger flips a fish he is in the process of gutting. To this abuser the little girl was not human and her agony heightened as he continued trying to . . . then the footage ended as the woman put the camcorder down and tried to help. No, not help the child, help the abuser.

That is child pornography, which I will be referring to as 'indecent images of children' from now on. Pornography itself is legal, and putting the word 'child' in front of it doesn't convey its abhorrence. Make no bones about it, the people who watch indecent images of children offend as gravely as the people who create them.

I'm writing this book to try and prevent your child ever suffering like that little girl.

1.

What is a Paedophile?

The paedophile is sexually aroused by children

This can take many forms – as all sexual arousal does – but the root of a paedophile's behaviour is the appeal a child holds for them in a sexual context. In my professional judgement and experience, a man does not need to have laid an inappropriate finger on a child to be a paedophile. He is primarily characterized as a paedophile by the workings of his mind, not his body. Any physical action he takes in the realms of paedophilia is secondary and stems from the fact that in his mind he is sexually aroused by children. So the first stage of the definition is his mindset, and the second stage is any action he takes – any action *he* takes. *He* decides on his actions; they are not decided for him. He can abuse or not abuse, he can watch indecent images or not watch indecent images, he can ogle children stripping off on a beach or walk away. A common misconception about paedophiles is that they are not in control of their actions and society should not expect them to be. I vehemently disagree. Paedophiles choose to act on their sexual attraction to children – nobody makes them.

In the next chapter I will look closely at 'grooming' – a sinister and calculated process designed by paedophiles to isolate a child ready for sexual abuse to begin. The time, imagination and patience that paedophiles invest in grooming shows how imperative it is to their success – but it also shows how totally in control they are. Over the weeks and months that a paedophile grooms a child, he will pass up opportunities to abuse until all his preparations have been completed. In simple terms, if a pervert can pass up opportunities and not abuse during the grooming process, then he can pass up opportunities and not abuse. While he is grooming he is turned on, he is alert and highly charged, he is savouring the coming moment when he can reap the months of investment and begin the abuse – but even amid the storm of this hormonal tempest he has the self-control to resist because the time is not right. *So he has the self-control to resist.* Paedophiles have to have immense self-control otherwise they can't groom a child, in order to abuse them later, in the first place.

Humans are powerfully driven by their sexuality. I believe God made it that way for lots of reasons – it keeps the world going round for starters. But however powerful our sexual drive, we never lose responsibility for it. If it was a biological fact that sexual urges cannot be controlled – as some paedophiles would have us believe – then there would be no basis for laws surrounding sexual conduct. It would be recognized that sexuality is beyond legislation as a bodily compulsion that cannot be managed, and we would all be free to behave with complete abandonment. But sex is not a force beyond us; we must all govern our behaviour and society rightly expects us to – including paedophiles.

The paedophile is in control

He is not a victim, he is not a piece of hormonal drift-wood helplessly tossed around by his feelings, and he is not a five-minute wonder who suddenly feels these irre-sistible urges once in a lifetime and then never again.

By the way, you will have noticed I am referring to the paedophile as 'he'. For the majority of this book I am going to refer to paedophiles as males rather than females. Men overwhelmingly occupy the world of paedophilia – though not exclusively as we will see later – so for the purposes of sensible reading I will use 'he' as I write instead of trying to pay deference to equality and tying myself up in knots. The use of 'he' is not intended to cause any offence to anyone, though admittedly I am not overly concerned about gender correctness in this context.

The paedophile is devious

It is part of being in control. He must maintain a façade of decency that does not betray his true motivations, and achieving that aim requires constant deception. Deviousness becomes a way of life for him; to sexually abuse a child there's a long list of people he has to deceive. For the best chance of success he has got to deceive the adults around the child into believing that he is safe to be left alone with them – parents, wider fam-ily, carers, teachers, neighbours, school friends . . . you get the gist. Then he has to deceive his own circle into believing that he is a thoroughly good bloke who would never do such a dreadful thing – family and friends, employers and colleagues. A particular ace card is fool-ing anyone in authority who could inadvertently assist him or vouch for him being a pillar of the community in the face of accusation. And, of course, the person he usually deceives the most is himself. We will look at the excuses and theories paedophiles concoct to make their activities palatable to themselves later in the book, but at their root they are all devious – they have to be. They couldn't abuse children if they weren't.

Accidents?

When I joined the police, more than fifteen years ago, road accidents were called road accidents. However, current statistics show that 95 per cent of road accidents are caused by driver or rider error and are not actually accidents at all, so they have now officially become 'collisions'. The word accident exonerates anyone from blame, because it implies that those involved were entirely helpless in the crash that occurred. Clearly the statistics say otherwise, and so the police have to refer to crashes as 'Road Traffic Collisions' to reflect the fact that they are invariably caused by error. So even accidents aren't accidents any more!

Likewise, the actions of the paedophile are not accidental, despite some of their protests to the contrary. They are in control.

I do not see how a person can accidentally sexually abuse a child. I have sat here and racked my brains for such a scenario but, with all my years of police experience discovering people in the most unimaginable of situations, I still can't envisage a scenario where an adult accidentally sexually abuses a child. Imagine the script: 'Oops-a-daisy, here I am alone with a youngster again, it's such a nuisance the way this keeps happening. I must make a mental note to be more careful who I end up in such compromising situations with, but while I'm here, I suppose I might as well make the most of it. This really is a most unfortunate turn of events.'

It's laughable really – well, it makes me want to cry too. Granted, a person might unwittingly find themselves in a questionable scenario with a child that was never meant to be what it looks like, but the right-minded adult doesn't grab the opportunity to commit abuse – they get out of that scenario as fast as they can. And as a mum, I can categorically state that helping a child with personal hygiene does not lead to accidentally sexually abusing them. That's another lame excuse paedophiles devise – that they were toileting or bathing a child and the subsequent sexual activity was an accidental part of a natural process. Every right-minded adult who has intimately cared for a child knows that that makes no sense at all. It takes motive and deviousness to sexually abuse a child.

Consent

An adult is always in a position of power over a child – intellectually, physically, emotionally . . . I'll spare you the list. The adult has responsibility for what happens to that child purely because they are an adult and the child is a child. It's not rocket science; it's nature. The only exemption I can perceive is where the adult suffers mental impairment, though that opens a new debate on the responsibility of the carer for that adult – and, for the record, I have never dealt with a case of child abuse where the perpetrator was clinically diagnosed as a mentally impaired adult. I recognize that such cases do occur, though for the purposes of this book I am discussing the majority of the adult population who do not suffer such impairment. The adult is always solely responsible – in law a child cannot consent to sexual activity. So let's bin the surprisingly prevalent myth that sexual activity between an adult and a child is excusable if the child 'consented' – *the child cannot consent*. This fundamental is so fundamental that the law enshrines it in the statute books. And which right-minded adult would want a child to consent to sex with them? Only a paedophile would want a child to consent to sexual activity or would create such a setting where consent is manipulated.

It follows that because a child cannot consent to sexual activity with an adult, any activity that does take place is abusive. It is always illegal, non-consensual child abuse. So when you read about a man who pleads some kind of sexual compatibility between himself and a kid as the grounds for activity between them, despair at his level of self-delusion and remember that he has violated that child. I do not accept any other explanation – *neither does the law* – and yes, I really do believe it is that simple.

Some offenders argue that the child made all the running. I denounce this on principle, but if the child appears to want something sexual to happen then that adult has more control than ever – not less. For a child to attempt to seduce an adult is a perversion of nature, and no decent human being would respond to such behaviour, let alone exploit it. You have to be a paedophile to see something so tragically unappealing in an innocent and rub your hands with glee.

Picture your kitchen for a moment: If I very reluctantly agree to bake a cake with you, you have a harder job of actually making it with me than if I had begged to be involved. The more keen I am, the more I will do for you; hey, get me to bake some extra cookies and do all the washing up while I'm happy to be so helpful! An apparently 'willing' child is more like putty in the hands of the abuser than a resistant one; they really are there for the taking. The notion of compliance does not justify abuse – it exacerbates the breach of trust. Further, if a child apparently instigates sexual contact with an adult, you've got to ask yourself 'Why?' A child is not naturally sexually overt, and for one to have become highly sexual suggests a measure of misuse has already occurred in their short life. For an adult to capitalize on that vulnerability is appalling.

The case of Mr A

Throughout this book I am going to draw on real cases I have dealt with and will conceal identities by referring to the characters by letters of the alphabet. Not very original – sorry – but hopefully straightforward.

Mr A was referred to our Unit by people who were concerned that he was using library Internet services to look at images of young boys. He was quite brazen about it, perhaps buoyed along by the stringent protection libraries have on their Internet facilities which meant he could only download legal images and technically remain within the parameters of the law. However, he was clearly spending hours staring at pictures of boys on the beach modelling items of swimwear and therefore the police were alerted. The material he was viewing was not 'illegal' but it was 'indicative' of an unhealthy interest in young lads. That is enough for us. Police obtained a magistrates' search warrant for his home address and we arranged to execute it early one cold and frosty morning.

We work in conjunction with another Unit to execute warrants as they are quite staff-intensive. Two of us take the offender away to the police station for questioning whilst another group remain behind to search the address and seize evidence. This usually consists of computers and linked equipment – cameras, disks, video cassettes, mobile phones and so forth – anything that can be used to make and store indecent images of children. We think as laterally as we can and that way we miss very little.

Mr A lived alone in a terraced house in English suburbia. In its 'niceness' there was nothing notable about the area – except Mr A's terraced house. It was abysmal. The rotted front door could not be opened because of the junk stacked up behind it, and the windows were blackened with grime – I could just make out that there were grubby rags of curtains hanging behind the glass but it was not possible to see inside. We had to use the rear door as a means of entry and, as my colleague hammered on the flimsy wood, I stared aghast into the back garden. It was so enormously overgrown it towered over the shed and was eagerly growing through the kitchen window into the house. Bearing in mind that our primary aim is to get our hands on evidential equipment, police do not allow people very long to answer the door before we boot it in. Every precious second is time they could be disposing of evidence, so after an initial warning the door hits the floor if the person doesn't open up very quickly indeed.

Mr A squandered his precious seconds turning off his computer. Just as my colleague was about to boot the door in – which he could have sneezed at to flatten – Mr A appeared at an upstairs window. He looked to be in his early fifties and was so unkempt that a tug through a hedge backwards would have probably tidied him up. My colleague reiterated that we required him to open the door NOW, but he still made no effort to come downstairs, so the door got it. That's when the nightmare started.

The rear door led into the kitchen – loosely defined, for it was unusable in its state of decay. The garden was encroaching its way along the sink, and everything was brown with filth. Broken and unwashed crockery was strewn over the surfaces, and so much rubbish was piled up between the cupboards that the room as a whole was inaccessible. We were in a hurry to get to Mr A before he disposed of the all-important evidence but our progress through the house was slow. The interior appeared as though he had travelled to his local dumping ground, compacted the contents into a garbage truck and then transferred them into his home. The mounds of rubbish were stacked so high and solidly that they filled the rooms up to the ceiling, leaving just a narrow walkway through the middle. At one point my sergeant tried to get past me but he couldn't squeeze by; we could only walk in single file and the junk was up around our faces the whole time. It stank! It was unnerving to think of all the bugs and germs scrambling into my freshly washed hair and riding on every breath I inhaled.

We struggled to find a light bulb that worked but, when we did, a part of me (the breakfast part) rather wished we hadn't. The light bulb's meagre beam illuminated the carrier bags of faeces and bottles of urine that were lying around as a toilet. The mice and rats, flies and insects were treating the place like a holiday camp. His bed was a mouldy mattress, his food a box of frozen fish fingers, and one of the computers was so encrusted into the floor we could barely remove it. Then suddenly Mr A appeared wearing a brand new suit and tie, and proceeded to politely introduce himself in the Queen's English to ask if he could help at all, officer.

On being swiftly arrested he was searched outside – the house too dim and cramped to complete it indoors. As we stood on his driveway I noted two dilapidated

cars he had parked there, both of which were unroad-
worthy and in the same hideous state as the house.
Mr A smelt so awful that we travelled to the police station with the car windows down, and he was followed
around the cell block by an officer armed with a can of
air-freshener. We took the decision to call a doctor out
before we interviewed him, to check on his mental state
and ensure he was physically capable of being held in
custody. He was evidently in great pain when he
walked, and struggled to traverse the short corridor
between the cell area and the interview rooms. During
questioning he made the usual denials and was released
from custody on police bail pending the forensic examination of the property we seized. To all intents and purposes Mr A was destitute, deranged and desperate.

The following week my colleague and I paid another
visit to Mr A's. We had reported his house to the
Environmental Health Department and, as well as carrying out some house-to-house enquiries, we wanted to
know if anything had been done to fumigate his address
or at least put the mower round the garden. It was conducting the enquiries with his neighbours that changed
everything. To our devastation, my colleague and I, who
are proud to be streetwise coppers whose eyes don't like
the wool pulled over them, learned the truth.

We were informed that Mr A owned a secret car
which he never parked it at his address. We searched
the vicinity and eventually found it in a small car park
– and were shocked to see that it was pristine.
Beautifully kept, it didn't have so much as a scratch on
it. It was everything we would have said Mr A wasn't.
Then we put some more of the puzzle pieces together.
The car was parked a fair distance away from Mr A's
address which meant he was obviously walking to and
from it; there was no other way to access its location. So

all that agonizing limping in the cell block was, at best, selective. As we continued our investigation, in time we were startled to find that the pristine car had been moved – he was obviously aware we had discovered it. This time it was parked in an empty supermarket car park, situated as far away from the store entrance as possible, neatly under the security camera. I don't know anyone who deliberately parks their car as far away from the store doors as possible, and the fact that it was carefully beneath the camera for protection suggested that this was now its new home. What was Mr A up to? Concealing a roadworthy vehicle and parking two wrecks on his drive, living in filth and maintaining an immaculate car, displaying signs of insanity while operating with precision, pretending to be lame when he was nifty on his feet . . . His deviousness shook us; we had not foreseen this turn of events.

When we first met Mr A he appeared to be out of control and at the mercy of madness, yet within his shambolic lifestyle he was very much in control, behaving with extreme deviousness and motivated by a sexual interest in little boys. For all his uniqueness, Mr A is a classic paedophile. Even the apparently out-of-control ones are alarmingly in control.

Behavioural groups

Every paedophile is an individual, but they do fall into behavioural groups in the way they conduct themselves. With the inevitable generalization that comes when you categorize people into groups, I am going to split paedophiles into four main brackets. You may be able to think of a case you read once that doesn't quite fit, but I've trawled the cases I know and can attribute all of them to one of the following groups. I'll start with the least common.

1. *Organized paedophile rings*

Ugh, the very phrase sends a shiver down your spine, doesn't it? Paedophile rings. You envisage this sinister group of slimy blokes sitting round a table beneath a dingy lampshade cooking up horrible ways to ensnare a child. I'd rather lunch with a pack of wolves than stumble on such a scene.

An organized paedophile ring is a group of child sex offenders who function together, motivated by their mutual desire to abuse children. They operate as a group for best effect, sharing skills and information and also sharing children. It is characteristic for rings to contain offenders with different preferences about who and how they want to abuse – that way they can share any opportunity to abuse that is created among them, and wring every day out of victims who fall into their hands. The man who wants boys but can only access girls will assist his friend whose preference is females, and the man who likes three-year-olds will pass his on to the man who likes five-year-olds when the child reaches that age. The man who likes five-year-olds will duly take his turn, then move the exploited child on yet again to the man who likes eight-year-olds as the years go by. The organization involved in operating so extensively while simultaneously evading capture is a mammoth undertaking. In the way they work, paedophile rings are as accomplished as they are repulsive though, thankfully, such an archetypal band of deviants working together to plot and execute child sexual abuse is a rare phenomenon. Still, when it happens, it is deadly. Often literally.

To be honest, I don't know why paedophile rings are as rare as they are, and I wonder if the Internet may slowly increase their prevalence. I'll tell you why I think so in a minute.

Some years ago, before my children were born, I was a detective in the Child Protection Unit. It was my job to investigate cases of hands-on child abuse being perpetrated by offenders usually known to the child and including sexual, physical, emotional and neglect-type abuse. I would interview the child or children on video-tape and then deal accordingly with the offenders – always working in conjunction with the Social Services and other agencies involved in child protection.

In the Child Protection Unit I dealt with a family that had been riddled with child sexual abuse for generations. It really was a case of taking the lid off the proverbial can of worms and unleashing the most terrible epidemic of woe. The investigation their tragic tale generated was complex, and widened out from the family to identify other local men involved in the crimes. And then some more local men, and then some more local men after that. I soon realized that the small and utterly dull locality that was hosting this case contained a seriously high number of paedophiles. I identified eight convicted sex offenders living in one street alone. Plus numerous children, of course.

Further enquiries showed that many of the pae-dophiles had a historical link to a sordid public house situated miles away in a town centre. Most of the links had been established for years, and names from the public eye that really shouldn't have been there began to appear in the jigsaw. Remember the bit about fooling people in authority who can inadvertently assist you? The paedophiles themselves were a mixed bag of indi-viduals – one was a vagrant, another was a sex offender who had numerous offences against children and adults (and he is still offending today). Not one judge has yet locked him up properly despite him having numerous convictions for rape and indecent assault. (I wonder if the judges would lock him up if he moved into their street? Just a thought.) Another paedophile owned the local toy shop and yet another was so police-aware he had a sophisticated system of cameras and security at his property so that we couldn't raid his house without him spotting us a mile off. You've got to be guilty of something if you're going to lengths like that!

There is no doubt in my mind that this locality was overwhelmingly populated with paedophiles by design rather than accident – and if I explained to you what a difficult job I had convincing my superiors that they really were there you would throw your hands up in disbelief. Believe me, they really were there. Sadly, although I always suspected the group was an organized ring I was never released from my workload to prove it. I was authorized to investigate those men whose crimes were reported to me, but not explore the activities of the others whose behaviour was gravely suspicious and crying out for proactive scrutiny. I do not doubt that I did nothing more than scratch the apparently genteel surface of that ring and will always regret that I was never able to delve properly into the extent of their operations. It's the usual story – offenders have far more time and resources than the enforcement agencies. The Child Protection Unit was – and is – intolerably busy, and we had an uphill struggle coping with the offences that were actively reported to us, leaving no available time to go searching for those that were not.

Systematic paedophile rings such as that bunch are rare, but the ones that exist are highly organized. Their computer knowledge and technological proficiency are second-to-none, and their clandestine communication methods, intricate planning, covering of tracks, and execution of offences are meticulous. A genuine paedophile ring is a terrifying group of determined men whose skill makes them notoriously difficult to convict. They are driven by a sexual interest in children, they maintain obsessive control and they are fearsomely devious.

Why do I think the Internet will increase their numbers?

Before I investigated indecent images of children I had obviously never accessed a paedophile website or chat room on the Internet. I was aghast to read the extensive amount of text that accompanies indecent images of children and to realize how graphically child sexual abuse is discussed among those who commit it. The sites were like another world, a safe zone where like-minded perverts could air-and-share their filth. It is revolting to read their conversations and to digest the fact that these exchanges are happening on a vast scale. I'm not talking the odd bit of writing jotted down here and there. I'm talking thousands of web pages constantly flying round the world from thousands of paedophiles gratified by reading each others' expressions of child violation. My personal belief is that these websites and chat rooms will unite paedophiles on an ever-increasing scale, and I miserably suspect that the upshot will be more rings of offenders bonding together than ever before. The Internet allows for such freedom of contact that working relationships between them seem inevitable to me; I don't have numerical statistics to support this – I just know what I've seen and the extent to which I've seen it. I guess only time will tell if I'm right or wrong – I pray it's not our children or yours that prove the theory.

2. Stranger-danger

The second category of offenders I am bracketing
together is perhaps the most feared of all: stranger-
danger men who pluck a child from the streets to abuse
them. This is a rare occurrence, but the fear of it is under-
standably widespread because on the occasions that it
does happen it is so calamitous that it *deserves* to be
feared. I don't think the burden of grief such offences lay
on the child's family can be expressed by the written
word. Although I know how uncommon the stranger-
danger paedophile is, I fear him as much as the next person.

A couple of months ago I was shopping in a small
rural supermarket with my two daughters. It was a
Saturday morning and we had completed the shop without too much strife. (By the way, have you ever tried the
'gingernut rule'? I have learned that if you give a kid a
digestive biscuit as a bribe to get you round the supermarket they eat it really quickly and you're doomed.
They bellyache for another one within seconds, then
they just bellyache for the sake of it and it's game over.
But gingernuts are great because they're so rock-hard it
takes ages to eat them and you've done a fair whack of
your shopping before the kids have even noticed.
Honestly, gingernuts last at least four aisles longer than
digestives.) Anyway, we were queuing to pay when I
realized that I had forgotten to get a packet of baby
leeks. I didn't want to lose my place in the queue and
neither did I want to go home without the baby leeks, so
I asked my daughters to go to the vegetable aisle and get
the leeks while I hung on in the queue. I reasoned that at
their age they should be pulling in little chores like that
and I should be trusting them to do so, especially
because they would only be out of my sight for a matter

of seconds. But that's the frightening bit – a matter of seconds is all it takes. I doubt the US President has better surveillance than the watch I mounted on their mission. Despite the tiniest likelihood of there being a predatory paedophile hovering by the baby leeks that morning I was on full alert, darting back and forth as I scanned their every move. I made sure I could see the CCTV cameras, the entrance doors, the ends of every queue, and both areas that covered the entrance and exit to the greengrocery section. That way I knew exactly who was walking past the baby leeks, what clothes they were wearing, where they went afterwards, and who they were associating with. My vision of someone carting the kids off was so real you'd have thought it was a fait accompli, not a national rarity on a par with UFO sightings. In fact, my behaviour was so bizarre I wonder now that I wasn't the one who was carted off.

Most paedophiles want to abuse a child for as long as possible and remain undetected. Snatching a little one from the street causes an immediate furore which doesn't actually help to serve their long-term purpose. They now have the dilemma of how to conceal that child amid the uproar and run a huge risk of being discovered on many fronts. Abusing a child as a stranger leaves the paedophile with limited control by default – he loses his grip on a lot of the events around him, and his ability to deceive suffers a hammer-blow. People are now on high alert for someone behaving just like he is and he has scant chance of duping them into thinking otherwise. The staple diet of a successful paedophile is not best fed by a stranger attack. For the record, I have never dealt with a 'stranger' child sexual abuse case, though I acknowledge, to my deep horror, that they do infrequently happen and with life-shattering consequences.

3. Family and friends

The third category of paedophiles is the one to watch most closely for, the most common by far, and that is the family member or friend who sexually abuses a child. They are as sly as they are prevalent, and can operate undetected for years. The outworking of their skill is multi-faceted and always boils down to supreme levels of control and deviousness in manipulating both the child and its circle into never disclosing, or observing, what is really going on. The person most likely to abuse my child is not the stranger in the supermarket but the man sitting on my sofa drinking my coffee. It's all about antennae.

In the local supermarket I am on hyper-alert regarding my children's safety. Both in and out of my sight-line they are encountering the unknown all the time, and anyone doing anything could be around the next corner. Behind our front door that alertness relaxes in me – yes, even in me! – and my antennae shuts down for a well-earned rest. No one comes into our home that my husband and I do not allow and so therefore no one comes near our kids in our home that we have not sanctioned. Our antennae are at best on stand-by, and our daughters' embryonic antennae are completely switched off.

Enter the paedophile. His mission is to keep our antennae from ever crackling into life, and he starts by summing us up through building a friendship. He's got to surmise what makes us tick so he knows how to fool us and hold us in the ignorance of our comfort zone. Once he has calculated how to secure such oblivion, he can go up a gear in convincing us that he is such a great guy . . . and gracious, he's so good with the kids! Look how patient he is when they jabber on at him and how he never forgets to shake their hands as well as ours.

Last week he even bought them a little chocolate bar each; how thoughtful. It may well take months for the groundwork to be properly dug and tilled by the paedophile, but he can wait, while all the time sowing seeds of assurance in us and of obligation in our child. For their part, the children subconsciously note our acceptance of him and place full confidence in the fact that Mum and Dad clearly think he's great. Whatever weird things he may progress to committing against them can't be that wrong if Mum and Dad think so highly of him. And when the weird things do start happening, a deep fear of reporting them and rattling the friendship cage Mum and Dad are happily locked into is a fatal deterrent for a child. Only when he is confident that he has secured the trust of us all will the paedophile move in for the kill.

It is not that different with family members, the main variation being that they often have an easier time getting started in the first place. The foundations of gaining access to your home and child without arousing suspicion are not so difficult to lay, and the expectation from family members is that blood-is-thicker-than-water and we are all looking out for each other. This wall of family strength is, ironically, the biggest barrier behind which a paedophile can hide. It should be the defensive barricade that protects the child but it is perverted into being the seat of power that condemns them. It permits the paedophile unquestioned access to the child and a persuasive threat to hold over them: 'If you ever tell anyone what is happening between us you'll destroy the whole family. No one will believe you, and everyone will hate you for ever.' What little one wants to carry that weight on their shoulders?

For a family member to abuse a child is so unthinkable that it is the easiest way to abuse a child. Put like that it makes horrible sense. No one in the family wants to believe it, no one wants to be so awkward as to guard against it, no one wants the fallout that results from its discovery – and that's if the child finds a way of reporting it at all. In Chapter 2 we will look more closely at how paedophiles can operate within personal circles. It is a chilling fact to absorb that your children are at the greatest risk of suffering sexual abuse within your four walls.

4. Internet offenders

The fourth category of paedophiles I have bracketed is offenders who use the Internet to view indecent images of children. These are arguably the most deluded bunch of all, because they manage to persuade themselves that 'only' viewing the images and not actually carrying out the abuse means they are not paedophiles. I do not buy that one bit. Of course they're paedophiles!

1. *They are sexually aroused by children.* That is why they are viewing indecent images of children and not adult pornography.
2. *They are in control.* Computers do not accidentally turn themselves on, enter passwords, connect to the Internet, search for child abuse websites, click on links, wait for web pages to download and trawl through material. That series of actions is a deliberate process by someone who is in control.
3. *They are devious.* Internet offenders do not view their filth in front of other people or chat about it on the bus. It remains a closely guarded secret stored behind obscure usernames, passwords, and solitude. A myriad of lies are told about what they're repeatedly doing on the computer, often late at night – 'You're not on that thing *again*, are you, dear?' – and deception is the

only way to perpetuate the addiction without reveal-
ing it.

Consider the TV show *Friends*. The reason it was produced was because the makers thought it would catch
on. Its content and characters were expected to hold mass
appeal to the general public and it was deemed worth
the investment. The makers were proved right when millions of people got the bug for it and tuned in to watch
each episode. This response from the audience dictated
what happened next. After the first series the producers
had to decide whether to make more programmes or axe
the show. Well, that can't have been a tough decision! The
programme is only worth the numbers who watch it –
and so *Friends* became highly valuable. Everyone who
watched it contributed to its production and facilitated
the long run of success it enjoyed. If no one had watched
it, they would not have kept making it.

It is no different for indecent images of children.
Internet paedophiles are involved in the making of all
indecent images and movies of children that exist – they
create and sustain the market. They are as responsible
for the suffering of every child they watch as the adults
who touch the children and activate the cameras –
indeed they are the fuel that powers the whole industry
and they have children's blood on their hands. The
viewer is just the final link in the chain of production –
but he is as significant a link as all the others who go
before him. Without his active support the world of
indecent images would stand a chance of dying out –
encouraged by his active support it burgeons on and on
with no end in sight to its agony.

Meet Mr B. He was investigated by our Unit last year,
and the initial shock was uncovering that he was a family doctor in a residential area. I don't know the exact

population statistics, but I have policed the area before as a front-line cop and can confirm that it has a high concentration of children among its numbers. Thus a family doctor working for that community will no doubt have a high proportion of children among their patients. This may well be why Mr B chose that particular surgery in the first place. To be a paedophile and a doctor for so many years without detection must by definition take tremendous levels of control and deviousness. I can't imagine how many people he must have deceived throughout his career – most notably his own family. You see, Mr B wasn't only looking at indecent images of other people's children; he was taking pictures of his own and posting them on the Internet for others to view.

I wasn't the officer in the case for this guy, but I do know that after he was arrested, forensic examination of his computer revealed a large number of indecent images of children. They covered the whole severity scale police use to grade images (more on that later) and they dated back many years – including the explicit photographs he had taken of his own family. He displayed an obsession with little girls' underwear, but was by no means choosy in that he possessed a variety of images of both boys and girls. His defence was pitiful and I will examine it more closely another time, but it was also original and indicative of a clever man who had prepared himself in case the day of reckoning ever came. As a copper, I am ashamed to say that the day of reckoning for most paedophiles invariably comes years too late – if it comes at all.

Paedophiles are found in every walk of life, manifesting their activities across a wide spectrum of offences, but at their core they are all the same. Take Mr A and Mr B. Outwardly they are the antithesis of each other: Mr A lived a lonely and destitute existence, while Mr B enjoyed the comfort of an affluent and happy home life. Mr A suffered some form of mental derangement – packing your house with junk while the garden grows through the window and carrier bags serving as toilets constitutes derangement in my book – while Mr B was a brilliant medic, as highly qualified as he was respected. One was very smelly and one was very clean, one lived a life of nothingness and one a life of noble achievement, one was destined to die unnoticed and the other to go with a respectable send-off.

But there are three identical features that tower over everything else when you look at Mr A and Mr B.

They are both sexually aroused by children. They are both in control. They are both devious. That is what makes them paedophiles.

You couldn't make it up

One morning a job came to us from a European police force that had arrested an adult male for running a child abuse website on the Internet. Individuals joined his club by sending indecent videos they had in their own collection to be posted on the site. That gave them access to all the other videos already contributed. It also allowed the pervert to believe that he was above the law because enforcement agencies can never send indecent material as part of a sting, for they would be committing the serious offence of distributing indecent images if they did. However, the man was not above the law and on his arrest the police removed a nasty indecent video from the website and replaced it with an innocuous one behind the indecent link. So the trap to catch far more offenders than just the one they already had was laid: the police picked off every user-name that clicked on the link, checked out the names with their Internet providers to identify the individuals and disseminated the details to the relevant police services around the world for prosecution. The statistics of this job alone are not nice reading; bearing in mind that this was one indecent video link on a website of thousands of such videos, on a worldwide web of thousands of such websites, the police clocked nearly three thousand hits in under twenty-four hours. That's the scale of the problem.

We promptly acted on the information we were sent and conducted an early morning raid on one of the suspects sent to us via this European investigation. The middle-aged male was hoisted from his bed and taken to the police station, where he made the usual denials pending the examination of his computer – which incidentally was later found to contain lots of indecent material, mostly pertaining to young girls. He shared the family home with his wife and stepdaughter, and so part of our enquiry extended to securing the daughter's safety in the light of the danger he represented. While asking Mum for names as I pieced together the family set-up, she referred to one as 'Stephen'. Scribbling away on my jotter pad I didn't look up as I naturally moved on to ask, 'Is that Stephen with a "ph" or Steven with a "v"?'

'I always spell it with an "S".'

2.

Grooming a Child for Abuse

I have an inner desire for fudge. No one else knows about it. They all want chocolate and that is quite normal. But chocolate isn't for me. I want fudge. It has to be of the purest kind, made exactly how I like it. I could go to the shop and buy some but it doesn't satisfy my urge. Shop stuff is full of preservatives and so commonplace that it isn't truly mine. Not to mention the harrowing stigma of being caught buying fudge – what a scandal there would be. My friends and family are so committed to chocolate that I keep quiet about my desire for fudge. Yet it is so strong I have to indulge it, I can't resist. I've tried to placate my needs by other means – raspberry liquorice, toffee bonbons, even yoghurt-dipped cashews – but to no avail. I have an inner desire for fudge that is so overwhelming I've decided to create some of my own. I'm going to make it here at home, right under people's noses, even using their precious chocolate to produce it. The challenge is to ensure they're none the wiser. I can rise to that.

Firstly, I'll hand the chocolate round a few times, take some myself and deign to eat it, and everyone will think how normal I am – just like them! Then I'll skulk off with the box. 'Hey, come back here, you!' I reckon one of them will yell after me. 'She's nicking all the chocolates, the sneaky rascal.' They'll think I'm desperate for chocolate and never guess what I'm about to do. If I wait long enough a few of them will nod off by the telly, others will go out for a walk, and I'll reap the rewards of my patience by finding myself alone in the kitchen. It'll be a two-edged sword scoring deep into my appetite; oh, the agony of the time spent waiting, but oh, the thrill of anticipating when I can finally get to work!

The moment will arrive and I'll undress the chocolate – pure and simple and mine to mould. I'll melt it down, ever so carefully so that it doesn't burn or suffer visible harm, then I'll add little tit-bits that I fancy along the way – maybe a few raisins or peanuts, all slowly mixing in with the butter and icing sugar to change the chocolate into my beloved fudge. It'll still look the same to everyone else – brown and square, smooth and tasty, pretty much chocolate really – but I'll know it's different. It's been moulded my way, to my taste, for my intents and purposes.

I must be careful as I work. If folk knew I was enhancing their chocolate they would accuse me of defiling it and be outraged. Defiling it! What a sentiment. If only they could feel the passion I feel and love fudge the way that I do they would understand. But for now they must never know. Outwardly the moulded fudge will give nothing away and seemingly be a chunk of chocolate as they have always known and loved it. I can mask the appearance of what I add and manipulate the raisins to sink below the surface where they can't be seen. I can keep the edges as pronounced as they expect them to be. And anyway, that's just it – no one is expecting anything. That's the beauty of it – no one is expecting such a shocking thing from me.

Then my greatest coup will come, my moment of triumph to be savoured: 'Hand the chocolates round, will you?' someone will shout when we're all gathered together. I'll hand them a chocolate, but right under their noses I'll have a piece of fudge for myself – and they'll be none the wiser.

The outworking of grooming

When a paedophile grooms a child for sexual abuse he befriends him or her in their natural habitat and mentally melts them down. Once he has destroyed the fundament- als of 'what' and 'who' they believe, he re-programmes the child to think and behave according to his own inten- tions, all the time building in allegiances to himself through fear, threats, gifts and the subtle smearing of fam- ily and friends. Such grooming relies on planning. The steady and calculated isolation of a child, coupled with the manipulation of the adults around them, is like con- cocting a recipe. You need the right ingredients in the right quantities combined with the right methods to pro- duce your end result. Chocolate doesn't often become fudge without the precision of a recipe and a child doesn't often become a sexually abused child without the precision of a plan.

As with paedophiles themselves, grooming is manifest- ed in countless different ways but the essential ingredients of a successful recipe are the same. I have summarized them into four main ingredients. Producing a condensed version of a complex subject invariably involves a meas- ure of generalization – but it is a small measure. Just before we look at the ingredients I want to clarify a few points about grooming and outline a real case I dealt with, to help put the ingredients into context.

It was as recently as 2003 that the process of grooming officially became an offence under British criminal law.

Put simply, the definition states that an offender must communicate with a child from anywhere in the world on at least two occasions and take measures to meet with them, in order to commit the offence. Prior to 2003 grooming was widely acknowledged to be the favoured method by which a sex offender prepared a child for abuse, but the law offered no protection against it and offenders had to progress into committing the planned abuse before the police could act. Thankfully, someone sensible suggested that if we prosecuted offenders at the preparatory stage, a proportion of them could be prevented from abusing – and child protection really could be child protection. Besides, to my mind, the systematic demolition of a child's thinking is, in itself, an abuse of that human being, independent of any other offences that may follow.

The outworking of grooming takes place in both the real world and the cyber one. The offender who conducts himself in person and the one who undertakes grooming on the Internet have the same mindset. The ultra-sinister edge I find the Internet holds over real life is its removing of the child from social awareness, and its ability to operate with absolute secrecy just that bit more than the guy who operates in the midst of other people. The Internet paedophile can close the child's world down; in person, the paedophile must conduct himself within it. Your child will not interact with an Internet paedophile on the computer while you're watching but they will interact with a 'real world' paedophile who has infiltrated your circle to target them. That gives you a chance to detect what is happening. And, of course, the ultimate edge of the Internet is the blanket power of deception: not many paedophiles admit to being a middle-aged man with a bald patch and a beer belly when they persuade a child to strip in front of the family webcam. They claim to be a youngster with similar interests and sexual immaturity, and the child invariably believes them. It's unnerving: we can all be anyone we want to on the Internet in a way that bypasses reality. In a later chapter we will explore what I consider to be the minefield of the Internet, and its power to have a far more detrimental effect on your family life than it can enhance it – or so I believe.

There is a strangely comical element to the deceptive power of the Internet. A common strategy for paedophiles is to inhabit children's chat rooms pretending to be a child. What they can never know for sure is whether the child they have engaged with and are fervently grooming is actually a child or another paedophile grooming them. That puts a wry smile on my face.

A serious case of child sexual abuse I dealt with in the Child Protection Unit was perpetrated as a result of calculated grooming. It is relevant to say here that the success of grooming is not down to the intellectual cleverness of the offender. Of course an abundance of brilliant brain cells helps the guy to think up more ingenious plans than his more cerebrally-challenged counterpart, but never forget that paedophilia is about being sexually attracted to children, maintaining control and being devious. You don't need intellect for any of those; you need determination, guile and patience. These two guys I'm going to tell you about were as lacking in the intellect department as the proverbial two short planks, yet they sustained the most awful abuse against their victim for years because they isolated her so thoroughly.

Mr C and Mr D were brothers. Mr C was married and had bullied his wife into complete submission from day one. Again, it is important to say that just as grooming is not about intellect, so domestic violence is not about muscles. Many of the men I have arrested for domestic violence offences have been as far away from a body-builder as I am from the moon. Their power over their victim begins as an emotional one asserted through fear and control, and their physical violence is a secondary action disseminating from that source.

Through his wife, Mr C came into contact with the victim, who I will call Lily, when she was twelve years old. Lily's home life was impoverished, exacerbated by Dad's alcoholism which squandered any precious pennies that made it across the family threshold. Mr C befriended Lily and purported to be the stable fatherly figure she was lacking. The bond she developed with Mr C and his wife deepened over the coming year, purposely fuelled by him, until they offered to welcome Lily permanently into their home and take care of her. *A year* – Mr C waited a year before he even touched her. What self-control he possessed. Of course Lily was delighted by the invitation, and Dad was even more delighted by the prospect of one less mouth to feed, so Lily officially moved in with the Cs. It didn't take long for Mr C to upgrade his attention towards Lily – he hadn't cultivated her all this time for nothing, he wanted to harvest the efforts he had sown – and he was soon committing sexual assaults against her on a regular basis. Her silence was easily maintained: 'If you tell anyone about me you'll have to go back and live with your dad. You'll starve there, no one will be your friend and Mrs C will reject you completely.' The grooming was reaping its rewards with every day that passed.

Mr D then entered the manipulated scene – entirely by design. Mr C had taken his turn with Lily on plenty of occasions; it was time to pass her on. Mr D became the shoulder for Lily to cry on as she struggled to cope with Mr C's abuse, and he offered to look after her instead.

'Come and live with us, dear, we'll protect you. Mr and Mrs C won't mind, I won't tell them anything and you can still be friends with them.' Relieved to be offered such an escape route Lily moved in with Mr D and his female partner, unaware that Mr D had been beating and raping his partner for years. This time the abuse towards Lily was immediate and far more serious than anything Mr C had ever done.

Mr D raped Lily frequently in every form, threatening her all the time with consequences of violence, rejection and homelessness if she reported him.

'If you didn't live here, who else would have you? Mr and Mrs C don't want you back, they're glad to be shot of you. Face it: life on the streets is far worse than you think it is under my roof. You don't get a meal on the table or a bed to sleep in when you're homeless.'

Lily was a desperate girl. The only way she could think of to escape her abject misery was to constipate herself so severely that Mr D would not want to be near her in an intimate way. So that is what she did.

One morning a file landed on my desk telling me to travel to a hospital a fair distance away and visit an eminent surgeon who was making a referral of child abuse. I made the journey and sat with this surgeon who informed me that he had just operated on a young girl with chronic constipation and its resulting problems. He had never encountered a case so acute, worsened by the fact that the symptoms were self-inflicted. Lily had been referred to the hospital by her GP who had seen her regarding severe back pain – it was Mr D's partner who had taken her to the doctor before the school could enquire about her poor physical state. The surgeon told me that Lily's bowel had been ignoring the messages her brain had been sending it for so long that the two had disconnected and were unlikely to ever reconnect. So, at the tender age of fifteen, he had fitted Lily with a colostomy bag and expected her to depend on it for life. If someone had spotted Mr C grooming Lily during that initial year, the lifelong nightmare she suffers today could have been avoided.

Lily and Mr D's partner fled to another town while I arrested Mr C and D. The upshot was that magistrates gave Mr C a slapped wrist for his abuse – I'm not sure what kind of lesson that was supposed to teach him – and Mr D went to prison for twelve years. At first that doesn't sound too bad, until you sit and think about it. English law says that the offence of rape carries a life sentence. Mr D committed countless rapes on a young and vulnerable girl, yet the judge gave him just twelve years instead of the numerous life sentences he was due. English judicial practice then dictates that prisoners who behave themselves in custody serve only half their sentence, and so Mr D was free to walk the streets after only six years imprisonment. He is currently on the Sex Offenders Register, and recent bulletins across our constabulary have flagged him up as 'high risk' and 'one to watch' because 'intelligence' states he is ingratiating himself with children again. What an ironic double-use of the word 'intelligence'. Common sense would say that he is going to ingratiate himself with children again – it doesn't take 'intelligence' to work that one out! I have no doubt that Mr D will rape another child soon – he may well be grooming his next victim now. Luckily for the judge, it probably won't be his precious babies Mr D targets.

How grooming is manifested

Ingredient 1: The target

The first ingredient in every recipe that changes chocolate into fudge is, of course, the chocolate itself. You can't use just any old chocolate, oh no. You've got to select which type of chocolate you want very carefully; they're not all suitable for the purpose. My long-suffering family know that all too well. I once attempted a new chocolate pudding recipe and scrimped on the quality of chocolate I was instructed to use. The result was a Martian-like gunge hovering nervously at the bottom of the bowl instead of the beautiful pudding beaming gloriously over the rim that the recipe had promised. The howls of dismay from my kids were totally justified.

'Yuck, Mum, that looks like a tummy upset! I'm not eating that. You can't even give it to the birds; it would be mean.'

The most important decision a paedophile makes when plotting sexual abuse is which child he targets in the first place. He is much less likely to succeed with the wrong child and it isn't worth the months of effort trying – it is time wasted that could be spent on the suitable child. What a ruthless decision. The callousness of this stage alone reminds us of the callousness of paedophiles; those who claim child sex offenders merely suffer from 'misplaced' or 'confused' feelings of love need to examine how paedophiles operate. In my experience paedophiles do not love the children they abuse: they approach them with ruthlessness before they even lay a finger on them – and then they destroy them.

In selecting a child for abuse the paedophile will look for a vulnerable place in their lifestyle or personality into which he can pour his poison. He's got to be able to infect them with his programme of new values and allegiances – if the child doesn't have an evident vulnerability through which he can operate he will usually prefer to move on and size up another target. The keyword here is 'vulnerability', which is not obviously defined. The evidently 'vulnerable' children in society are the very young, mentally impaired, already abused, victims of poor parenting and so on. The not-so-evidently vulnerable children can appear rock solid, but if the paedophile detects a weak spot in their set-up he will attempt to infect it. In a way I guess every child has a weak spot – it's part of being human – but these are some of the common ones he will look for

- *A child who is being bullied in any form*. The bullying produces a catalogue of needs in the child that the paedophile is only too willing to fulfil.
- *Puberty*. Every paedophile has ridden the hormonal rollercoaster of puberty and so they know how easy it is to manipulate tender adolescents trying to be older than they are and longing for someone to tell them that they are gorgeous.
- *A child lacking parental attention*. This is not always as a result of bad practice, but can be the result of heavy work commitments, the demands of other siblings, the strain of illness and so forth. The way into this child's life is obvious, and tragically two-fold. Because the child is lacking in adult attention they latch on to the friendship that is offered, and because the child is lacking in adult attention no one notices.
- *Children passing through crisis*. This can happen to any child at any point and cover a whole spectrum of scenarios, notably marriage breakdown which can also result in a two-fold vulnerability. One is the emotional upheaval of the split – all those tumultuous

feelings of disturbance, divided loyalty, misplaced blame; there's a well of weaknesses to be plundered – and the other is the potential for Mum and Dad to meet new partners. That subsequently introduces a whole new family of strangers into the home, and I am sorry to write that step-relatives are the most common offenders who commit familial child sexual abuse. I once dealt with a lady whose husband had left her and their young daughter. She was a lovely lady, very switched on, and well supported by her family. A few boyfriends came and went, all decent guys apparently, when one day the little girl marched up to the latest chap, undid his trouser zip, and asked he if he was going to play the 'jungle game' the last bloke had taught her with his 'snake'. Mum's disbelief was almost as deep as her distress.

Those are just four common vulnerabilities: by default the list is endless; that's the bad news. But the good news is good – it's very good! Knowing how paedophiles hunt for a child's weak spot gives every caring parent the opportunity to introduce the necessary safeguards to strengthen that weakness as much as possible. As a mum I know that I must understand my children better than anyone and, through that knowledge, both educate and protect them in the areas where they are weakest. As with every child, my own daughters have vulnerable places in their characters – and I am going to get to those places first. I'm not leaving them exposed for some monster to come along and beat me to it. It takes a bit of painful self-analysis as well. I don't like looking at the many mistakes I make as a mum – but if I don't and an outsider does, then I've lost. I cannot be too aware of how my life and lifestyle, my temper and my shortcomings impact on my kids, and when I see that wounded expression in their eyes that tells me I've messed up again, I determine to learn the lesson so that no one can come along and teach it to me the hard way.

The most basic weakness in children has got to be sweets. If your child doesn't have a weak spot for sweets you deserve a medal; oh boy, *I* have a weak spot for sweets. My children love them and would be drawn to their delicious colours by someone trying to lure them away. I can either despair at the thought and just hope it won't happen, thus leaving the weak spot weak, or I can infill it with my own set of values and toughen it up. I've decided on the latter. I frequently tell my daughters that good people who are strangers know that they mustn't tempt kids with sweets, so anyone who does do it must be bad. They *must* be. I have programmed them to automatically think, 'You are offering me sweets. I don't know you. You must be bad.' Bit of a generalization I know, but I can live with that. I've conjoined that rather blanket announcement with the winsome promise, 'If ever anyone we don't know offers you sweets, you say "no" to them. You come home and tell me about it, and I'll buy you whatever sweets you want.'

They haven't spotted the mileage they can get out of that one yet, but I guess it is only a matter of time.

Ingredient 2: Relationship

Once the paedophile has selected his child and the weak spot through which he is going to access their lives, the second ingredient of his recipe involves building a relationship with them. There are two vital elements to this, which can either be established separately or in conjunction with each other.

1. He needs a *trusted* relationship with the child and the adults around them.
2. He needs to get that child *alone*.

Those two words are the important ones: *trusted* time *alone*. The lengths a paedophile goes to – sometimes incredibly detailed and time-consuming – are all about creating time with a child that no one asks awkward questions about and no one sees. The woman from the 'jungle game' case trusted her new boyfriend. He was so thoughtful that every Sunday morning he told her to lie-in because she deserved it, and he would take the little girl out of her hair for the morning. Without realizing what he was really thinking she *trusted* him *alone* with her child.

In my opinion, the biggest clue to someone grooming your child is if they are pressing for trusted time alone with them. It's so imperative to the execution of sexual abuse that it is an ingredient the paedophile cannot omit or cut back on. He has to create the time alone, and will find a myriad of ways to do so. Sit and think about the adults who have trusted time alone with your kids, especially those who have engineered it. Sit and think about the adults who advertise for trusted time alone with your kids, then add the adults whose professions give them trusted time alone with your kids and suddenly the net is cast far and wide. Of course it doesn't render any of them sex offenders – but it is one of the best routes to your child.

A few months ago our youngest daughter was due at a friend's house after school, and I realized that the dad was going to be collecting them. That made me wonder if he was going to be looking after them on his own at home as well – a situation my husband, John, and I have always said we will never allow. Apart from my dad, no bloke ever looks after our children alone. I rang the mum and was honest with her (risking possible offence) and she assured me she would be at home with the children the whole time. The following day, the dad approached me in the playground and, before I could apologize for any offence caused, he said he was pleased I had asked the question – it reminded him of how he should watch out for his own daughter. And then he summed up: 'At the end of the day, any parent knows you have got to put your kids first, before upsetting anyone else. You haven't upset me, quite the opposite. I admire your vigilance and have had a wake-up call from it.'

Paedophiles can't abuse your children in front of you; they've got to get them off your hands before they can get their own hands on them. If someone was gunning to be alone with our daughters, constantly coming up with ideas and persuasive reasons about why we didn't need to be around, our antennae would be crackling so intensely we'd burst into flame.

Ingredients 3 and 4: Creation of allegiance and establishing of secrecy

The third and fourth ingredients in the recipe are closely related: the creation of allegiance to the paedophile and the establishing of secrecy. As adults it is too easy to look at these issues with our maturity – but paedophiles aren't that short-sighted. They know that a child's commitment to loyalty and secrecy is differently won to an adult's and so their plans are tailored accordingly. Sometimes I have dealt with cases and wondered how on earth the child fell for such a story and kept the secret against the odds – then I realize I've fallen into the trap. That's it: they're a child. It's different for them.

To transfer the allegiance of a child away from its strongest relationships onto a third party is no mean feat, and further testimony to the patient skill of paedophiles. They manage to break down the whole existence of the child so far and the way they have operated: telling Mummy or Daddy the most basic of events, chattering to friends about whatever they're thinking. I wouldn't tell a child the time if I didn't want the whole world to know it, yet paedophiles trust the child with their darkest activity, and in doing so they trust them with their liberty. That's how confident they are in their own ability to re-programme the child's thinking – a child who betrays them sends them to prison, so it's only when they are confident that the transfer of allegiance has been fully achieved that they will begin the abuse. Paedophiles risk everything in abusing children – that's how devoted they are to abusing children.

The transfer of allegiance is tested along the way to ensure that the recipe is working. Relatively innocuous situations are instigated that can be easily backed out of without raising suspicion, yet they reveal an awful lot to the paedophile. Let me give you an example: when I was a kid we were seldom allowed sweets – I saw snow more often than Smarties. If a paedophile had been grooming me, he would have fed me Smarties and told me not to tell my parents, warning me about the trouble we would have incurred on discovery. That's an immediate and compelling threat; to 'tell' would bring trouble on my own head (never nice) and also the head of this kind gentleman buying me precious treasure in the form of Smarties. Now he can test me. A week later he can ask if I have kept the secret. If I haven't, he'll feign ignorance about the Smartie ban if my parents confront him, even blame me for not coughing to it: 'Gracious me! I'm so sorry. I'd have never offered her any if I'd known. Isn't she a little monkey, not letting on?'

He now also learns that I am not a safe bet in the secrecy stakes and moves on to consider a different child. For a paedophile who thinks he's getting somewhere this process will happen over and over again before the abuse starts and, by its subtle nature, it is difficult to detect. By the time the abuse does start he is assured of the child's allegiance and secrecy, and they are already steeped in 'wrongdoings' he can hold against them: 'If you tell Mummy where I've put my hands, I'll have to tell her about all the Smarties you've been eating recently and lying to her about. You'll be in so much trouble.' That's a powerful hold to have over a child.

I can't think of a case that illustrates the heartless creation of allegiance and secrecy more graphically than the one I am about to tell; sadly, the offender was never prosecuted. I was told about the abuse when the victim herself had survived into adulthood – yet her loyalty to the offender was still so entrenched she would not pursue a formal complaint against him. This is as common as it can be confusing in cases of child sexual abuse. The natural response of a survivor would seem to be the pursuit of justice, revenge, even punishment driven by the deepest bitterness, but often that is not so. The foundation of allegiance on which the abuse was built can endure into adulthood, long after the offences have ceased. And, if it is a foundation the paedophile has laid firmly enough, it is not readily shaken. Pity, protection, excuses, duty, fear, compassion – they all emanate from it and conspire to keep the survivor loyal to the offender. If the child has been sufficiently isolated and led to believe the offender is their only friend, that offender becomes their whole world as well as their abuser. The abuse is marginalized into just one aspect of a special relationship the child believes they cannot live without, and that deep undercurrent of allegiance can often last a lifetime unbroken.

Here is an example of allegiance and secrecy.

The little girl was one of eight children born into a severely dysfunctional family. Mr E was unemployed and unemployable, and Mum was so lacking in her own ability to conduct basic tasks that the toddlers had more gumption than she did. In fact the budgie had more gumption than she did. Due to a poor diet and heavy drinking, Mr E suffered from bad health, and this became the basis of his recipe. In their frenetic household it was difficult to secure time alone with anyone, so to create it he began feigning particularly bad health in front of the child he had selected. Of the eight kids, she was the most caring and it was for this 'vulnerability' he chose her. Right on cue she showed obvious concern for his demonstrably ailing health every Sunday afternoon. Mr E allowed this to grow, exaggerating his pain, loudly worrying about imminent death, and ruthlessly generating great sympathy in the terrified child. She reached the point of believing Mr E was going to die imminently, maybe before her very eyes. What could be done to save him?

One afternoon Mr E led her upstairs – trusted and alone – and confided in her:

'Poppet, no one else knows this, not even your mummy. I trust you because you're so special. The doctors have told Daddy that he has a terrible disease called appendicitis and I need a special treatment once a week to help me. If I don't get the treatment I'll die. You're so lovely that you're the only one I can ask for help – but you mustn't tell anyone. I don't want to worry the others, especially your mum, but for as long as you treat my

appendicitis the doctor says I won't die. It'll be our special secret, just you and me. If you tell Mummy, she'll
cry. Will you save me from death, poppet?'

Her allegiance and secrecy were secured from day one
by transferring responsibility on to her for the very mor-
tality of Mr E. If the child did not co-operate, she would
cause her dad to die. Years of Sunday afternoons followed where the girl could be found upstairs alone with
Dad, tending his appendicitis and saving him from
death. Then one day at school, she learned that a man's
appendix isn't part of his groin.

As an adult she never lost the weight of responsibility she had been burdened with for Mr E's welfare. The
very telling of the story filled her with guilt that she had
somehow let go of her culpability and pulled the trigger
on his life. Mr E was an incompetent man – but he maintained control over that child in the midst of a packed
family home and beyond, into adulthood. He was devious. He manufactured trusted time alone with her for
years, and he built a solid foundation of loyal secrecy
that endured long after the offending did. Without any
other talent to his name, Mr E was an accomplished paedophile.

A dangerous diary

Imagine I am a thirty-two-year-old male. This is how I
would infiltrate your family and begin grooming one of
your children for sexual abuse. My diary has recorded
the recipe.

Saturday 10th Jan
A new year . . . and a new family have moved into number twenty-one. I didn't mean to stare at them when I

opened the lounge curtains, but I couldn't help watching the children dashing about the overgrown garden while Dad tried to cram too much junk into too little garage space before shutting the door. What striking kids – two of them blond and one with a long dark mane like a stallion. I'm spoilt for choice . . . Only one way to resolve that, I need to find out more.

Sunday 11th Jan
I strolled down to the paper shop earlier when Dad was out on the lawn – I wandered past him (not the most direct route, but he won't notice a detour like that) and nonchalantly threw a 'Good morning!' at him. He was eager to return it – thought he would be – and before long we were chatting like old buddies. What a goldmine of information! Flo is the eldest at twelve years; Mickey, the middle one, is ten; the dark stallion is actually a girl called Jen, but oh, that wonderful hair. Flo and Jen are clearly the apples of Dad's eye; you'd think Mickey would be his golden boy, but apparently he's too wayward for that which tarnishes his shine. Notable.

Wednesday 14th Jan
Mickey was out on his bike today – I just watched from the shadows of the lounge. I don't think he saw me – why would he be looking? He rode up and down the street, doing wheelies, and appeared completely unsupervised. It was precisely twenty-eight minutes and forty-three seconds before Mum came to the door and yelled at him to come in for his tea. And did she yell! Not a trace of kindness in her voice. Mickey was in the house like a shot; he danced to her tune all right. Notable again. It's amazing what you can pick up by watching, just silently watching and reading the signs.

Saturday 17th Jan

I have never resented rain like I resented it today. I was planning to go outdoors and mingle with my new neighbours but the rain that has kept them inside has kept me inside. I haven't forgotten little Flo and Jen, it's just that Mickey has generally been out and about more than they have . . . and I like the out-and-about type. He's the one Mum and Dad most want out and about too, which makes him the one for me. He is their headache which makes him my tonic.

Tuesday 20th Jan

Progress! The rain can come as much as it wants to, because Mickey's mum has a leaky pipe which I spied on for a few minutes and then ventured out to assist with. She was so grateful – right on cue – and equally as forthcoming as her husband about her unruly brood. Clearly Mickey is the tearaway and as such he is mine. I offered to play a bit of football with him – right outside the house where anyone else can join in (though I know they won't want to) and she said the magic words, 'Oh thanks, but you don't have to do that. He'd be thrilled if you did, but don't feel obliged.' I assured her I wasn't obliged and exaggerated my involvement at the local club – promoted myself from occasional visitor to part-time trainer – and that was it, more magic words, 'Well, to be honest, what with the move and work we've not been able to help him along with his football, so yeah, thanks, that would be great.' Mickey is obviously the child who gives them the most trouble, and so he's the one they most need to have occupied. Far from worrying, she's glad I'm going to keep him company. Got him!

Saturday 24th Jan

Just when I thought I was doomed, my day came together! I hung round the front garden as much as I could to draw

Mickey out, but nothing! Just as I had weeded the last weed that wasn't there anyway, he waltzed out the front door, football under his arm and surreptitious glances in my direction. An hour and a half of very public football later and I have learned that he can't have chewing gum – cousin choked on some once – parents are always busy, he's banned from watching James Bond films, and longs for thick football socks like the professionals wear. No problem!

Sunday 25th Jan

That was close, not like me to be so slack. I was walking back from the paper shop carrying *The Times* in one hand and a multi-pack of spearmint gum in the other when Mickey's dad came out to wash the car. Managed to pocket the gum as we chatted, and he thanked me for coaching Mickey. I told him it was a pleasure, that Mickey had talent – he didn't get my meaning – and I invited him to join us next time. His answer was exactly the one I hoped for, would have backed off if it hadn't been: 'I'd love to, but with all the stress of moving and the pressures of work, I'm just really grateful to you for giving him the time. I'll cheer him on from the terraces when he's playing for United!' He added that he wanted to take me for a drink to say thanks for sorting the leaky pipe.

Mickey and I played in front of the whole street for a while, until I deliberately knocked the ball that bit too far over my own garden fence. For cosmetic effect I made him ask his mum if he could come with me to collect it and she was fine – knew she would be, but notable – and soon we were stranded alone in my conservatory. Wasn't my fault I couldn't find the door key! Wasn't my fault the gum fell out of my pocket! I ate some and feigned bad memory when he suddenly asked for some.

We agreed to keep it as our little secret and he had four pieces at once, even trying to blow bubbles with it while I found the key. He was only with me seven minutes, but they were very profitable ones.

Wednesday 28th Jan
Thought not: Mickey hasn't said a word about the gum. Parents didn't mention it when I briefly said hello, and he confirmed our secret when he rode by on his bike. Time for the next stage: bought a set of James Bond films and a compendium of 'Training Little Football Heroes' by ex-England managers. Later went out for that beer with Clive, Mickey's dad, and three hours of talking, two rounds of pool, and five pints later we are mates for life. Too easy – all that in exchange for one leaky pipe!

Saturday 31st January
I called in to see Clive over lunch, had a natter about the footie on telly this afternoon, then watched him fall into my trap like a mouse sniffing for cheese. I asked if I could 'borrow' Mickey for ten minutes – he didn't flinch at the word – just said I needed a young lad's opinion on a design I'm doing for work. Thought I'd better offer to let Clive come too, was sure he wouldn't though, and he didn't – likes his footie and a bit of space from Mickey too much. But Mickey came along no problem. He had more chewing gum and a few chunks of strawberry bubblegum too. While he was looking at my designs on the computer I left James Bond running on the TV – knew he wouldn't be able to resist peeking, and he didn't! I made sure it was a violent bit – no point him watching boring stuff – and he was mesmerized. We strengthened our pact not to tell about the gum and the Bond films; his eyes were aglow when he agreed it. He's loving this as much as I am. Do I hold tight here for a while, or move on to the next stage?

Sunday 1st February

Yesterday's dilemma was taken out of my hands when Clive played right into them. Mickey called at the door saying Clive had sent him! He wants company down the pub later. I don't really fancy it, but the investment value is too great to miss. Mickey happily came in for a lemonade when I asked him and watched another ten minutes of Bond – this time a sex scene. I observed him carefully. He was well into the action, loving the naughtiness, and proud that I treated him like an adult who enjoys these things. This time it was him that told me not to tell his parents – definitely ready for the next stage.

Tuesday 3rd February

I *deliberately* returned the gloves I had *deliberately* forgotten to give back from Sunday's pub jaunt, just now. I also *deliberately* returned them when Mum – must start calling her Ali – was frantically trying to cook the tea and do twenty other domestic chores at the same time. I calculated it perfectly. Ali was so distracted that she begged me to sort out the over-boiling pasta while she fathomed Flo's maths homework and answered the phone. I never expected an invitation into the bosom of the family like that. Good work – especially as Clive wasn't even home. Better than that, I soon realized Mickey was alone upstairs and so I was able to lay more groundwork in the next three minutes than if I had had ten bags of cement over my shoulder. Of course Ali accepted my request to use the bathroom with a flick of the hand towards the stairway, and I used the bathroom all right – with the door wide open and a curious Mickey staring on. I pretended not to notice him, but I could feel his gaze, and made sure he saw as much of me as possible. The pretence continued when I acted shocked to find him watching, even cross, but his horror-struck face alarmed me even more and putting my fingers to both our lips I mouthed the words, 'Another little secret, soldier?' to which he nodded with relief.

'Mum would kill me. Sorry, mate,' he said and began retreating to his room.

'Hey, no sorrys between me and you, soldier. I don't shut the door in my house – and when you visit, you don't need to either. And as long as you don't tell anyone you won't get us into trouble. Us boys have got to be boys! James Bond Boys!'

'Yeah!' he smiled, giving me a 'high-five' and following me downstairs. Oh yeah!

Wednesday 4th February

Mickey's mine for the taking. He's nicely hooked on the end of my line; I just need to steadily reel him in. Mustn't go too fast, but mustn't lose momentum either. Clive and Ali are hooked up too, mainly because they'll take any childcare for Mickey they can get, but I don't quite know enough about them yet to move up too many gears. Mickey knows I treat him differently to the way they treat him – and he prefers my treatment. Lots of attention, contraband sweets and films, naughty bathrooms – how much trouble would he be in if his parents knew what a disobedient boy he is away from home? And if I need to I'll ratchet it up by accusing him of nicking the gum and damaging the videos – who are they going to believe? I haven't sweetened him with the promise of thick football socks from the United shop yet, I haven't asked Clive if Mickey would like regular football training, and I haven't watched Mickey in my bathroom . . . yet. But I will. The groundwork is laid, the defences are being built, and the prize awaits me at the end.

Mickey's all mine!

You couldn't make it up

One Friday night some friends were out on the town when they were approached by a gang of yobs and mugged. The usual loot was stolen – mobile phones, wallets, watches – and the muggers made good their escape. Unfortunately their success went to their heads and they committed another mugging a short time later, but this one fell foul of the law. An alarmed passer-by witnessed the incident and rang police who were on the scene within moments. A couple of the fleeing muggers were not light enough on their toes and were soon collared by the pursuing officers who attended. The muggers were also not smart enough to have ditched their loot from the earlier offence and still had the stolen items in their possession.

Once the muggers were in custody, the police had to return the valuables to their rightful owners and so scoured the mobile phones' data for clues as to who they belonged to. In doing this they quickly found that one of them was full of indecent images of children and so they passed the phone on to our Unit.

In the handset we identified a home number for the owner and rang the guy to happily tell him the good news: 'Glad tidings old chap, your muggers were caught and your stolen mobile phone has been found. If you wish to call in at the police station, we would like to return it to you.'

He did and we didn't – he called in at the police station, but we didn't return the phone to him. We arrested him for possessing indecent images of children and then raided his home address and seized a large amount of further equipment. (Oh, and the muggers were convicted of robbery as well!)

3.

Policing and the Courts:
The 'Justice' System?

In my experience, the English Criminal Justice System does not contain much justice for victims and survivors of child sexual abuse. It more often compounds the suffering already endured by these brave people who rightly expect the law to contribute a measure of healing to their pain. If you think I am speaking too strongly in this chapter, I assure you I am being as polite as possible. If I wrote what I really think about the justice system, as strongly as I really think it, there would be so much smoke billowing from these pages you wouldn't be able to decipher a word. Policing pornography – predominantly indecent images of children – is an evocative job, and when you spend your days watching children being brutalized, you cannot help but feel passionately about their human rights above all other legalities.

The main perspective I write *this* chapter from is as a copper in the Paedophile Unit investigating indecent images of children, though I do also draw on my years spent in the Child Protection Unit dealing with all aspects of child abuse being committed by offenders in person. After that I write as a Christian, a mother, a woman, a human being, and a defeated optimist.

Pornography: it is the strangest world I have ever encountered. It's an underworld, a secret world, and yet it is one of the biggest businesses on the planet. And, if I may say so, I think it is more of a bloke thing than a girl thing; to be honest, I've always found the mainstream material I see at work rather boring. After a few episodes of functional activity I find myself thinking, 'Oh hurry up, get her kit off and just get on with it, will you?'

Pornography is a developing habit that does not often remain on a level. Those who use it adapt to what they see and then need new stuff, crazier stuff, nastier stuff to provide the kicks. (There's going to be lots of possible innuendos in this section – if you try not dwell on them, neither will I!) On my first day in the Unit, a colleague was watching some seized videos in the viewing room adjoining our main office. The door to this room was directly behind my desk and all I could hear coming from the viewing room was 'whack, mmm, whack, mmm, whack, mmm'. Intrigued, I spun my chair round to see a huge female backside, which was being repeatedly walloped, filling the television screen. At first I was shocked by the sight – not having watched a spanking video before – but it soon became mundane. Two cheeks accompanied with 'whack, mmm' over and over again only has so much potential, and I realized that if I had been gratified by that video my gratification would have been short-lived before I would have needed the action to have gone up a gear. The material people start off viewing is rarely satisfying them weeks later, and the line between what is legal and what is not legal is easily crossed.

It is this principle that leads some offenders into viewing indecent images of children who would once have sworn they would never do such a terrible thing. The Internet has no boundaries and offers limitless temptation to those already entrenched in pornography; it's like wading into quicksand. Once you're in, it's got you. The indecent material grabs the instincts of some men, and they are dragged into its filthy world offering little resistance. Driven by the sexual addiction that renders them so hungry and willing, they progress from mainstream adult images and go looking for material that increasingly shocks and excites and horrifies. Note: *they go looking*, no one makes them. The adult becomes a teenager, the teenager becomes a child, the child becomes a baby, the naked pose becomes a gang rape, the gang rape becomes abuse-to-order via webcam from an offender who has a child present with them. Reality is lost in the deception of the Internet as the viewer sinks deeper and deeper into the quicksand. I believe that some offenders do not start out seeking indecent images of children when they first use pornography, but the powerful current of the quicksand draws them in – *and they choose to let it*.

Offenders always have a choice; they remain in control of whether they walk away or not, of whether they seek help or not, of whether they progress into illegal material or not. Whatever the psychology of their addiction, there is never any justification or excuse for involvement in child sexual abuse – never. The quicksand feeds on an instinct already in them – if it wasn't there it couldn't feed. Millions of adults use legal pornography for years without being drawn into child material. You have to have a weakness towards the perversion to even consider viewing the sexual abuse of children, let alone actively logging on to websites and enjoying it. Whatever route a man takes to reach the quicksand, it *becomes* him once he gets there. If he is watching indecent images of children he is now a paedo-phile and the journey behind him is irrelevant.

When he arrives at the most depraved image and it not longer satisfies him, the only avenue left is to find a child and begin abusing them in person.

What is legal?

So, what is legal in the world of pornography? It's prob-ably easier to say what isn't. These next few pages come with a health warning: I will choose my words carefully, but the gist will sometimes be unpleasant, so don't start on your lunch just yet.

Regarding adult material, the legal line is basically drawn at the word 'obscene'. But that's such a subjective definition that I find it next to useless. Last year I seized some adult material involving extreme violence which was describing itself as 'sexual masochistic pornogra-phy'. Personally I couldn't see what was sexual about the content at all – apart from the fact that the violence was meted out on people's private bits I failed to regis-ter what 'sex' had to do with it. I wanted to prosecute the offender for his depravity but was not allowed to; the slicing and beating, the burning and piercing did not constitute 'obscene'. Not even when the offender wrote about how much he wanted to abduct, torture and mur-der a young female – that apparently was just his fanta-sy world to which he was entitled. So perhaps I'm not the best person to explain the legalities of adult pornog-raphy to you. If I'm honest I don't entirely understand them myself.

The obvious material that inhabits the word 'obscene' contains corpses, animals . . . I know, unbelievable isn't it! It is hard to imagine how anyone can indulge in making or viewing such things but, horrifyingly, there are armies of people out there who cannot push the boundaries of obscenity far enough in what becomes a futile search for gratification and, in doing so, they immerse themselves in material that most other people could not entertain in their worst nightmares. The long-term consequences for these armies is scary; filling your head with such horror – more and more of it without being satisfied – can surely only destroy you in the end.

Aside from viewing child images, my worst case scenario happened three months ago when a colleague and I had to watch a number of home-videos a man had taken of himself engaging in sexual activities with animals. It was sickening beyond words, and my colleague and I were both troubled by viewing it. The man's acceptance of what he was doing when we later arrested and interviewed him was equally as disturbing, aggravated by the way he admitted to cajoling his wife to join in the action. I questioned him about why he had persuaded her to do so and his staggering reply was: 'Our marriage was going through a bad patch and I thought it would help.'

Most people see a counsellor.

My mechanisms for coping with images of depravity is a subject I'll explore later, but I do want to emphasize here that the only way I managed the repulsion of the above videos was through my faith in God. I do not know how my colleague filed the horror away in his memory – all I do know is that I didn't file it in mine. I returned home disturbed by what I had seen, and I prayed. It was the only guarantee of removing the vileness. However much the man above plumbed the depths of degeneracy, God's beauty is always deeper, and it was to this assurance that I came. I had (silently) prayed 'The Lord's Prayer' at the beginning of the taped interview with the man, aware of the revolting discussions I was about to engage in, and I had (also silently) asked God to deliver me from the evil and surround me with his kingdom, his power and his glory. Yes, even there in that crummy police room talking to a depraved individual about unspeakable things, God was irrefutably God. This is his world, every corner of it, and I relaxed into his authority in that interview room just as confidently as when I attend church on a Sunday. God is not defined or contained by bricks and mortar, and my testimony is that I experience the reality of God just as powerfully at work among the filth of my job as I do inside church buildings. There is nothing elitist about God. He has immeasurably vast resources, and after work on that day I simply asked him to turf the revulsion out of my head and clean my mind with his peace. I cried a bit, I talked to John, I prayed a few more times and it was over.

The law regarding indecent images of children is clearer than that pertaining to adults. A 'child' is any person under eighteen years of age – not sixteen as commonly thought – and 'indecent' generally begins at nudity and ends amid the same abhorrence as above. 'Image' includes still photographs, moving films and pseudo-photographs where offenders manipulate originally legal pictures into appearing indecent. Naked children are obviously not offensive in the daily routines of life, but photographing them undressed brings people to the boundary line. Honing in on their modesty or sharing such pictures around catapults them across it. Images of naked children found in an adult's possession always have the potential to lead to that adult's arrest – whether or not there is anything otherwise sexual about them. So much is subjective when defining indecency: images of a naked toddler can be innocuous to one person, innocent, sweet even, but they can be lethally arousing to another. The law rightly allows that an image of a naked child can be illegal – and then the responsibility is on the individual to defend the image if necessary.

My first ever case in the Unit was referred to me by another police force who had arrested a sex offender distributing indecent images of children to hundreds of other people. Everyone involved was identified by their email addresses waiting patiently in the man's computer – paedophiles are usually so wily, yet they can only really cover their own tracks and never be entirely sure how the tracks of their contacts are faring. We catch heaps of perverts through identifying their mates; I think of it as 'job satisfaction'.

The original offender had sent one image to Mr F, and it was of a little girl lying on a bed with her underpants on. Technically it was a legal image. The girl wasn't naked, nothing sexual was taking place, and to all intents and purposes it could have been a holiday snap. But why was a paedophile sending it to another adult male? In that context the photo crossed the boundary line. On applying for a search warrant at court I argued that although it was not 'illegal' the image was 'indicative' of an unhealthy interest in children, added to which it was being distributed to Mr F by a proven paedophile. Thankfully the magistrates agreed with my argument and granted me a warrant to raid Mr F's house, primarily on the strength of one image that in many contexts was acceptable. His computer later revealed a collection of indecent images of children that were much more serious.

I never change my children on the beach, I never photograph them naked, and I never allow them in the garden undressed. I have seen too many voyeuristic websites that are devoted to illicit pictures of other people's kids doing innocent things to chance the exposure of my own. The very thought of my kids being beamed round the world for perverts to drool over is not one I can describe without profanity.

The main reason police officers have to view indecent images of children is to grade them in terms of their severity for prosecution purposes. Images regarded as more severe receive a greater sentence on conviction at court – well, that's the theory anyway. Police categorize images according to a levelling system called the 'Copine Scale' which I will outline shortly, but first there is one fundamental difference between adult and child material that I want to stress. If I wrote this fundamental difference in capital letters, underlined it, put into italics, and accompanied it with flashing lights and a trumpet fanfare it would not be stressed enough:

ADULT PORNOGRAPHY IS ACTED
CHILD MATERIAL IS REAL

No doubt there are some adult actors whose participation in pornography is a miserable and enforced one, and I want to recognize that without exploring it. What I must stress is that the children who feature in indecent images are victims suffering real-life abuse. They have no choice, they are not acting, they are being defiled by those who make the images, those who watch them, and those who find excuses for those who watch them. *The abuse of children is not an entertainment industry*. Every image is the real and indefensible violation of a child – whatever its severity and whatever facial expression the child has been told to display. A child smiling for the camera is not a happy child; it is a child too terrified to disobey instructions.

This is how the Copine Scale works. (You need to hold off from eating just a little bit longer.) Images are graded from level one to level five; level five representing the most serious. Police have to look at every image found in a computer – however many thousands there may be – and grade each one according to the following criteria. It's a time-consuming and horrible task.

1. Level one images are of naked children, often in erotic poses but not exclusively so.
2. Level two images relate to children committing sexual acts of any nature with other children.
3. Level three images refer to pictures where children are shown behaving sexually with adults, excluding penetrative acts.
4. Level four images are those showing children in penetrative sexual acts with adults.
5. Level five images are of children portrayed in the extremities of this awful world – sadism, bestiality, torture and so forth.

I am often asked how cases of indecent images are referred to the police in the first place (it's safe to tuck into your lunch now, by the way). The most routine source is other police forces worldwide that have dealt with an offender and found numerous other contacts lined up in his computer. Any identified as living in our force's area are sent to us to investigate. Those jobs are great because the intelligence is foolproof; we simply go to the Magistrates' Court with the information, and they invariably grant us a search warrant to begin a new investigation. This usually writes another chapter to the story, because that person's computer will often contain details of yet another group of offenders he is communicating with and on it goes. It's a nice story, isn't it! Lots of perverts chatting to each other and leading each other to the police.

Other sources of referrals are the discovery of images by a third party in a computer someone has been using – either at home, at work, at a friend's house or, as with Mr A from Chapter 1, a public place like the library or an Internet café. Many jobs come to us as a result of police operations on the Internet or checks made by credit card companies or Internet providers. One came to us via a burglar who had been casing back gardens for a property to ransack and peered through a window to see a man watching indecent images of children on his computer. The burglar was so outraged he rang 'Crimestoppers', which is a free telephone line for reporting crimes anonymously. I don't know if he went on to burgle the place or not, though I doubt he nicked the computer! A few come from the police Child Protection Unit who deal with an offender who has committed abuse against a child in person and then is found to possess indecent images as well.

The case of Mr G

Last year I dealt with Mr G – his case is a relatively standard one and from start to finish it exemplifies how the police prosecute paedophiles viewing indecent images of children. Please keep in mind that my views on offenders, the Crown Prosecution Service and the courts may not coincide with yours, but they are formed from years of firsthand police experience which has never reconciled the sterility of the justice system to the reality of injustice.

The initial information came to the police through 'Crimestoppers': an unknown person gave Mr G's correct name, age and address, before adding that he had indecent images of children on his computer. By their anonymous nature such reports have the potential to be malicious and we strive to corroborate any information given before acting on it. After confirming that the personal details about Mr G were accurate, I spent a day trawling through various police systems and archives to see if I could add any meat to the bare bones of the 'Crimestoppers' report. Through the Child Protection Unit records, I established that Mr G was known to police and Social Services for heading up a complex and crippled family network, riddled with complaints of child abuse that had never been substantiated. They had always been withdrawn by the children who had made them, and no formal action had been taken against Mr G.

That issue is a difficult one to call. The police need evidence to prosecute a case and, in this area, children are the primary source of evidence, though even in cases where the child has co-operated fully with telling their story, the judicial rules are stacked against them and cases fail more often then they succeed. Therefore when children are not forthcoming, the police stand precious little chance of prosecuting the offenders. It sounds so cold-hearted, and it is. In my experience, the courts do not allow children to be children; they require that, however much they have suffered, they conform to the mechanics of the legal process *or are dismissed*. I hope that one day the justice system overhauls its methods to show proper respect towards victims. Their voice has been an irrelevant one for too long when surely it is the most important. To me the courts operate as though barristers and defendants are of more value than victims – I've never worked that one out. It is the victims who show the courage, who take the risk, who bear the suffering, whose lives are plundered, who live with the consequences, who pay their taxes, *who are the point of the whole exercise* – yet the disrespect with which they are trodden on at court promotes the advancement of legal professionals and the protection of offenders. The justice system is far from a level playing field, but without the courage of victims and witnesses, there would be no court process at all.

Among the wealth of complaints against Mr G was a statement made by a teenage girl about unwanted attention she had received from him years earlier. Again the girl had made the statement and then not pursued it, but three lines in the middle of the seven-page statement were gold dust to my case. I cannot stress this enough: 'not pursuing it' is not equivalent to retraction. Her story was never withdrawn as untrue, she just felt unable to stomach the court process. Enough said. The girl stated that Mr G had made her watch indecent images of children on his computer. That was all I needed – independent support corroborating the 'Crimestoppers' information – and I sat down to prepare an application to the courts for a warrant to search his address.

The applications are requested under specific acts of legislation and, after completing the extensive paperwork, I attended the court and nipped in to see the magistrates before their trials began. We see them in a back room that is completely private, and after swearing the oath of truthfulness I presented my information to them and asked for the warrant. It is very rare that they do not grant them – we're not so daft as to make weak applications that they're likely to refuse. Once the warrant was granted I had a limited time period in which to execute it, and planned to do so early one morning the following week. The early hour is timed to catch offenders before they go to work and, in the interests of discretion, we wear jeans and T-shirts and drive plain cars. Though I must say the discretion bit is a slight paradox – ultimately we cannot conceal the fact that we are six strangers raiding a house and carrying away people's computer equipment, so in that respect I don't suppose we're very discreet at all.

I have to admit that I love the moment when six of us stand outside an offender's front door about to drop a huge bomb into what he expects to be a routine day. I think of the children whose agony he has perpetrated and I savour my job; these few seconds are a rare smidgen of justice which is great to witness. We ring the bell, we hear his footsteps inside with perhaps a cursory, 'I'll get the door, dear,' then it swings open and he looks at us quizzically. We introduce ourselves with a quick flash of our warrant cards and he's still confused – until we say the magic words '. . . and we're from the Paedophile Unit.' I love that moment; their facial expression is the most compelling admission of guilt I know, coupled with an instantly dry mouth that can barely speak. The innocent are perplexed, the guilty are horror-struck and you know straight away if you've got your man. Either way, we enter the house empowered by the warrant and get our hands on the evidence before anyone else does.

There is one tragedy about executing warrants and that is the families. It must almost be on a par with a death message for them when a group of coppers invade their home, seize their property and announce that their beloved is a paedophile. Most have lived in blissful ignorance prior to that rude awakening and, as much as the offenders have absolutely no sympathy from me, their families have huge amounts.

We discovered Mr G living with an eighteen-year-old girl who, to be frank, looked more like a thirteen-year-old (with a well-developed chest), and had a personality to match. He referred to her incorrectly as a relative. The house was awash with computer paraphernalia, and as my colleagues began their meticulous search Mr G burst into crocodile tears, accompanied by loud cries along the lines of, 'Woe is me, they think I'm a paedophile!'

This amused me no end because we were trying to be discreet and he was declaring his true colours to the neighbourhood. I couldn't have put it better myself . . . well, come to think of it, I suppose I could have tried. A colleague and I took Mr G to the police station – where yes, of course he denied everything – while the rest of the group seized the evidence to be stored for forensic examination.

Mr G was released on police bail that day, while his equipment was analysed by the Police High-Tech Crime Unit. This Unit is a relatively new dimension of policing that specializes in examining computer and mobile phone data. It's staffed by both police officers and civilians, all of whom are incredible whizzes with computers and useless at making the tea. They're like sophisticated sniffer dogs in the way they search through equipment and find whatever is there. No matter how cleverly the offender has stored his information, the Unit are always better, and if there's stuff to be found they find it. But Mr G wasn't clever! He had saved his indecent material in computer files with his name on, and had taken indecent photos with his own mobile phone which had captured the distinctive tattoo on his arm. So his illegal data was not only traceable through the Internet records, but had been neatly saved and organized into document files which clearly identified him. He proved his own case for us! But what Mr G lacked in intelligence he made up for in depravity.

In time the computer analyst searched through every computer drive Mr G owned, ignoring the legal data and copying the illegal stuff on to an evidential disk for me to work with. The analyst locates the indecent images and records where and how he has located them – he doesn't have to scrutinize and level them. That said, the High-Tech boys see as much pornographic repulsiveness as we do, and yet manage to retain a vibrant sense of humour. Mr G was found to have an extensive and hideous collection of child material covering all five levels of the Copine Scale, and relating to children of both genders and all ages. It took me days of horrible viewing to trawl through every image and movie, but by the end I was able to prepare twenty-two serious charges against him.

Police no longer decide their own charges for any offences – the Crown Prosecution Service do. We approach them with the evidence we have collected and the CPS decide whether and what to prosecute. The lawyers who make the decisions generally sit in offices at the police station and don't venture out. That means they don't meet victims or defendants, and are governed by strict targets, objectives and budgets when making their decisions. I find it a huge worry.

Imagine being the CPS lawyer with a rigid dictate of overwhelming success to abide by. Your bosses have made it clear that you cannot risk pursuing a case that carries much margin for failure, so effectively at this embryonic point of the justice process you must assume the role of judge-and-jury by predicting the outcome. If a case is a dead cert you can proceed; otherwise you can't risk it. Within such tight targets there is little room for chance – not financially or statistically. The majority of cases are not inevitably won but need to be fought for, and so the best way around the predicament is to dismiss the weakest ones and reduce the others – for example, a serious assault is charged as a minor one which is more easily proven. The reality behind the national conviction rate is that it rides on the back of many cases being dismissed or reduced; sadly it is not saying that lots of offenders have been found guilty of their full crimes, as the statistics would have us believe.

My twenty-two charges against Mr G were initially agreed by the CPS but soon 'streamlined' down to a far lesser number. I wondered why I'd bothered spending days looking at his filth and preparing detailed schedules of every image when, in the end, the offences were lumped together into vaguer charges that only painted half a picture. During police tape-recorded interviews, Mr G's emphatic defences to the charges had been laughable – and I'll detail them in Chapter 8 – but on the strength of the reduced charges he suddenly ditched his months of denials and pleaded guilty.

Let me write that again. When the charges were robust Mr G pleaded 'not guilty'. When they were greatly weakened he suddenly remembered that gosh, yes perhaps he had viewed some indecent images after all and he pleaded 'guilty'. Lesser charges carry lesser sentences, but he still gains the benefits of a 'guilty' plea while the CPS still get a 'conviction'. Everyone's back is scratched and the case is closed. But to my mind he hasn't pleaded guilty – not properly, only to a diluted version of events that bypass what really happened. Mr G's guilty plea was not authentic justice. It was 'trial-by-budget' that prioritized time and costs ahead of the truth.

The 't' word. The truth. Diluted admissions are a dilution of the truth as well as a dilution of justice. The truth didn't feature with Mr G; I didn't once hear it mentioned and at court I rarely do. Witnesses are berated with the consequences of telling lies, but the establishment itself seems to ride roughshod over the truth. From what I have seen of the legal profession, lawyers are not primarily upholders of truth: they are brilliant performers who manoeuvre the letter of the law to meet their clients' needs. There's often an element of truth built into the manoeuvre, but it's not the priority. As a precept at court, it is my belief that the truth is a hitting-stick for witnesses, a celery stick for the CPS, a pogo stick for defence barristers, and a sherbet stick for defendants. *But the truth should be the yardstick for everyone.*

I was outraged by Mr G's diluted form of justice; the CPS scratched the surface of the truth, picked a portion of it and was satisfied. I wanted to fight the original charges but this was not on their radar. We had a 'conviction', targets were met, budgets preserved . . . and that seemed to be what mattered. Oh, and along with the truth, the children were never mentioned either. They seemed to be irrelevant. Justice for Mr G had nothing to do with the victims of his crimes. It was more about bargaining one judicial detail against another, until everyone had what they wanted – the CPS walked away with their conviction and Mr G got away with as much as possible. A compromise was reached by the interested parties – and they weren't principally interested in the truth or the children. I'm sorry to say that that is entirely normal; there is nothing unusual about Mr G's case.

Months after Mr G's 'guilty' plea we all gathered at Crown Court for him to be sentenced. Just before this took place two issues suddenly arose. The first surrounded a movie that I had categorized as a 'level five' film – Mr G was not prepared to plead guilty to it. The content of the movie was technically level 'four'; a three-year-old girl was being raped and screaming for mercy while trying to pull away from the clutches in which she was being held. Mr G was only prepared to accept the video as a 'four' and not a 'five' – though he was prepared to accept it! I argued that the child's distress constituted 'torture' and on that basis I had rightly upgraded it to a level 'five' movie. Mr G's barrister argued that irrespective of her distress, the actual content of the film was a penetrative act, which is 'only' level four.

'Irrespective of her distress'. As far as I was concerned we were there *because* of her distress and thousands like her, but, by his own admission, the barrister was functioning irrespective of her. I rest my case.

By showing the barrister the film in question I won that point and the film was accepted as a 'level five'. But my cheeriness soon evaporated. Mr G's barrister then announced that his client had just remembered he was abused as a child and needed adjournment for psychiatric reports to be prepared that could affect the sentence. Now I really was furious! I had interviewed Mr G a number of times throughout the enquiry and he had never said a word about this, despite lots of other defences being offered. The investigation had taken months, and we were to believe that up until now he had had no recollection of the trauma of childhood abuse that conveniently came flooding back just as he was about to go to prison.

I found it disturbing that court time and costs didn't dictate the response to this development. Despite the enormous expense and inconvenience, the professionals who had attended the sentencing were turned away for costly psychiatric reports to be commissioned. Mr G's rights were honoured with no regard shown to the public purse – if only his little victims were shown the same respect.

When he was finally sentenced, Mr G was sent to prison for one year. He had hundreds of indecent images of the severest level, from teenagers being gang-raped to toddlers being tortured. Under English law he will only serve six months of that sentence. By the time you read this he will have been out of prison for a while, popped to his local computer store on the way home and reconnected to the Internet before so much as putting the kettle on. His

sentence was fleeting and, for a man so addicted to indecent images of children, I imagine it was a hazard worth
risking. His many years of offending were not reflected in
his short sentence – let alone the lifetime of agony for the
children whose abuse he has savoured. I simply do not
understand such futile sentences. That one was next to
pointless. It did not reflect the crime, it did not respect the
victims, it did not protect future victims, and it offered the
barest minimum in terms of punishment, rehabilitation
and deterrent. The sentence rendered the justice system
worthless to me, and I work for it.

When I was working in the Child Protection Unit, a
judge delivered his verdict on one of my cases with a
staggering contradiction that summarizes the injustice
of the court system to me. The abuser had just been
found guilty of seven years of sustained cruelty against
a twelve-year-old girl – yes, she was just five when the
cruelty started. It covered a wide spectrum of physical
assaults (beatings, hurlings down the stairs), sexual
assaults, and cruel acts like being force-fed mouldy food,
kept awake all night, put outside in freezing temperatures and encouraging her siblings to urinate on her bed.

The judge announced, 'This is the most sadistic case
of child cruelty I have seen.'

'Yippee!' I thought. 'A judge who understands. It's a
terrible case and now at last the abuser's going to get
what's coming to him.'

Then the judge continued, 'This is the least sentence I
can give.'

Pardon?

The judge went from acknowledging that it was the
worst case he had encountered to seeking the *least*

sentence he could give. My brain still cannot understand that concept all these years later. For seven years of sadistic cruelty against a young girl, the offender was sentenced to four years in prison but he only served two of them. That told the child that she didn't matter and that the truth of her suffering carried little weight. She was old enough to understand what had happened and quietly told me that the court had hurt her as much as the abuser had.

The Register

Upon his release from prison, Mr G will be required to abide by the conditions of the Sex Offenders Register. The police have statutory obligations placed upon them by the government to assess and manage the offenders on the Register. The simple part of this is to ensure they comply with their registration requirements, and the complex part is to assess their level of risk and prevent re-offending. Note that we all recognize they present levels of risk; no one is pretending they don't.

All offenders on the Register are required to keep police updated with their current name, address, foreign travel plans and any other travel that takes them away from their home address for seven days or more. Different offences and lengths of sentence determine the amount of time an offender must register these details, but it ranges between two years and a lifetime. Popping to the police station occasionally to update these particulars is not onerous for paedophiles, and it does not prevent child abuse. It enables the authorities to keep track of offenders in the simplest form; it is certainly better than nothing – but not far from it.

Once initial registration has been completed, the police then have to risk-assess the offender to gauge the likelihood of him re-offending. 'Horse', 'stable' and 'bolted' spring to mind here because surely such an assessment should be made before we release an offender – not afterwards? The assessment is conducted in conjunction with other professional bodies, principally the Probation Service and Health Service, and then other agencies like the Youth Offending Service, Immigration or Housing Department, as necessary. A set of guidelines called the 'Risk Matrix 2000' steers the assessing officer through the key features of an offender's history and, dependent on how he scores against these guidelines, an offender is assessed as being of 'low', 'medium', 'high', 'very high' or of 'critical' risk to the public. (Scoring 'critical' does not send the offender to prison; it just alerts the police that a strike is imminent and someone's child is about to have their life decimated.)

The offender is now fully registered. His required details have been logged, and it is his responsibility to keep the police updated. His level of risk has been assessed according to the Risk Matrix and, whatever he has scored, he is living in the community. Various agencies are responsible for monitoring the offender, all towards the ultimate goal of preventing him from re-offending. For the vast majority of the time he is unmonitored – the process at best amounts to a weekly meeting with probation and a therapy session – but for most offenders it is a lot less than that. Those deemed to present lower risk can pass their time on the Register completely unchecked. No agency has sufficient staff to do otherwise; we are all hopelessly outnumbered.

I thought I'd leave you to make up your own mind about how effectively the police manage sex offenders on the Register. I'll lay out for you how it works in the force I belong to and you can conclude whether it is an effective form of protecting children and deterring paedophiles.

My force isn't the largest in the country, and there are about seven hundred paedophiles registered on the Sex Offenders Register. Hundreds of abusers who have never been discovered will be actively abusing in the county, and plenty more who have not been convicted will be known about by the police. Others will be convicted offenders who have done their time on the Register and are no longer required to abide by it. These seven hundred are just the ones we have formally cautioned or convicted who are still within their required years of registration.

There are four detective constables whose job it is to run the Sex Offenders Register and they are overseen by a detective sergeant, though plans are in place to add another detective at some stage in the future. Mathematically, that currently means each detective constable has 175 offenders to monitor. The detectives work 5 days a week for 8 hours a day. So, of the available 168 hours in every week, they are at work for 40 of them – that's 23.8 per cent. Therefore the registered paedophiles are officially unmonitored by police 76.2 per cent of the time. When the detectives *are* at work they have many reports to write and constant meetings to attend with the agencies outlined above. The majority of police time is taken up with these activities – I'd say at least 70 per cent of it, which is 28 of the 40 hours detectives are on duty. That leaves them about 12 hours per week to engage with offenders. So, the crude maths of the Sex Offenders Register in our county results in 4 detectives having 12 hours a week to monitor and assess the 700 paedophiles who are registered; 175 each in 12 hours is 4 minutes per offender – and these calculations haven't allowed for travelling time, annual leave, officer sickness, or lunch breaks. How effectively do you think the Register works?

The essence of the Sex Offenders Register is commendable, and certainly every little helps. It's better to
keep tabs on offenders than not keep tabs on them – but
understaffed and overworked Units maintain such negligible tabs that the Register can degenerate into a toothless bluff. To be effective the Register needs to be run
with more staff and more power – the ability to mount
more comprehensive surveillance, to conduct frequent
searches, to seek custodial extensions, to delve deeper
into offenders' activities – basically to remain one step
ahead of abusers instead of trotting along behind them
sweeping up the messes they leave in their wake. Child
Protection doesn't protect very often. It tends to see the
offence coming, watch it happen and clear it up afterwards. The law doesn't allow for much else.

There are no easy answers about what to do with paedophiles once they are proven to be child abusers. The
Human Rights Act empowers them with the same
respect as their victims, and current sentencing policies
in this country seem loath to lock them up for any length
of time – if they are locked up at all. Therapy and rehabilitation programmes are available but, as with all
public services, they are over-subscribed and under-
resourced. The worst offenders are prioritized for these
programmes, and then the success of the treatment rests
squarely on the willingness of the offender to co-operate
and be rehabilitated. The odds on that are not great. Just
as you can lead a horse to water but not force it to drink,
you can lead an offender to a rehabilitation programme
but you cannot force him to rehabilitate unless he really
wants to. For example: in the spring of 2007 the
Northern Ireland Prison Service released figures showing that only 12 of their 153 jailed sex offenders were co-
operating with treatment programmes. The remaining
141 – over 90 per cent – were refusing to attend, and yet

were still free to leave prison after serving only half of their sentences. The figures also revealed a glaring lack of professionals available to deliver the programmes at all; only three forensic psychologists applied for six vacancies advertised by the Service.[1]

Of the 700 registered offenders in my force, detectives know that a significant majority will re-offend. Child sexual abuse is what those offenders do – take Mr D from Chapter 2 who groomed Lily. Thanks to intelligence reports our whole constabulary knows that he is a convicted child rapist who is freely hanging around children again. We all know what he looks like, where he lives and what his name is. We know that he will strike again and none of us are doing much about it. It's not that we don't want to; it's that we don't have the time or resources to watch him twenty-four hours a day. The best we can do is keep a random eye on him and wait for him to strike. Then we will throw all the staff at him we can! A bottomless pit of money is plundered through the police, solicitors, probation, therapy, prison, Social Services, psychiatric teams, medical services . . . if only we could afford to prevent offences like we can afford to deal with the aftermath. And that's before we consider meeting the needs of the violated child.

The best way?

I wish we could hold those offenders that we know are about to strike again in custody. The consequences of their actions are so catastrophic I think we need to prove that they are safe before they walk the streets – not let them walk the streets and watch them prove to us that they are not safe. It's a controversial opinion until your child is in the firing line, then it's not such a bad idea.

I think the rights of the last victim and the rights of the next potential victim should be featuring in release decisions ahead of the rights of offenders. A victim's right to privacy and safety is as fundamental as an offender's – personally I think more fundamental – but rarely given legal consideration. Just stop for a moment and think how much a victim's privacy is raided when they are sexually abused . . . and what is the Human Rights Act doing about it?

Locking paedophiles up may not be the best way of dealing with them as people, but the law says that the protection of children is paramount – and locking paedophiles up is currently the best way we have of protecting children. But that's where I believe the law gravely contradicts itself, as our legal practices do not often adhere to upholding the protection of children as paramount above all other factors. Budgets, targets, resources, bureaucracy, politics and offenders' rights often shout louder than the children. The police are so limited because convictions are hard to secure, and relying on children as your primary source of evidence in an unforgiving system is not conducive to justice; the courts are so limited because their agenda is alien to child protection, and even when a humanitarian judge wants to send a pervert to prison he is prevented from doing so by strange sentencing policies and overcrowded jails; the Probation Service is so limited because they have a large number of offenders to be managed by a small number of staff – 'lip-service' is often the best service they can provide; rehabilitation programmes are so limited because the vast majority of offenders do not want to co-operate with the therapy that is offered, and no incentive is built into sentencing to confront their refusals. The prison service has to be where the buck stops. Surely it's at least worth a try if the protection of children really is paramount? It's got to be better than the rampant epidemic of child abuse ravaging our country; the current system simply isn't working.

Yes, I know the age-old argument of the jails being full to bursting and there's nowhere to put them all. *Which only goes to prove how many there are and how urgently our children need protection!* Call me simplistic, but if we added up the cost of each paedophile offence incurred through the above agencies – in both dealing with the offender and with his victim – we amass a vast sum of taxes that could be put towards new prisons and preventing the offences happening in the first place.

The justice system's primary duty of care in this land should be towards the innocent but, as a police officer with many years' experience, I have watched it transmute towards the guilty. I think the system is gutless and I'm ashamed of it.

Oh, just to finish the story . . . this morning Mr G telephoned my office from prison asking for his computers back. The gall of the man! His solicitor had forgotten to tell him that destruction of his equipment is integral to his conviction and besides, if I gave him his stuff back I'd be guilty of distributing indecent images to him and be due a spell in the slammer myself.

You couldn't make it up

When I was at school I had the customary life aspirations that many youngsters have; maybe I'd be a teacher or a bank manager, and I'd like a husband and some kids along the way. I never dreamt, or hoped, that watching the extremes of pornography would feature in my employment, and therefore also never dreamt that I woud ever send a text like the following to my husband.

Last week I sat down to watch one of several crates of videos seized from a man suspected of using his camcorder to record children in public toilets. It was necessary to view all his video cassettes in an attempt to discover any indecent images of children, but they consisted entirely of either extreme adult pornography or trains – the child indecency was confined to his computer. I am still deciding whether watching three hours of 'Merrily to Marylebone' is worse than three hours of masochism. After a while, they seemed to be on a par with each other.

Feeling particularly sick as I viewed the porn, I sent the following text to John

> What am I doing here? At the same time I am watching one video where a woman is being sexual with vegetables, another featuring a man who is physically halfway to becoming a woman, and another where a group of sadists are being very sadistic with each other. Call me old fashioned but whatever happened to a box of chocs and some flowers?

Endnote

[1] Data from *Belfast Telegraph* Thursday 31 May 2007.

4.

Churches: When Sacred Ground Becomes Hunting Ground

Between 70 per cent and 80 per cent of characters on the Sex Offenders Register attend church. This is a widely accepted estimate drawn from interviews held with the characters themselves. The figure itself is terrifying, and then there remains the possibility that the other 20 to 30 per cent lied when they were asked the question. After that we have to take into account the sex abusers attending church who are not on the Register: the ones who haven't been caught or reported, the ones whose victims couldn't face the court process, the ones whose convictions have failed, and the ones who are no longer subject to the Register's conditions. The church is a magnet for paedophiles – I hate saying it, but it seems to be true. It also seems to be true that the church is an ill-equipped magnet, which is the most terrifying bit of all.

My father was a church minister, and I have been part of one church or another all my life. I am proud to be a Christian – my faith is who I am and my commitment to Jesus Christ will never change. I believe that Jesus died to redeem humankind, and when God raised him to life three days later, every evil imaginable, even the power of death, was defeated by the authority of God. Jesus is innately compassionate and forgiving, and the Christian faith centres on the unconditional welcome he offers all people. Churches are right to seek to emulate him as they open the doors of his house to his people – and everyone on this planet is included in the phrase 'his people'.

There is another dimension to Jesus Christ which is just as important. Jesus is no mug: he cannot be conned, he will not be mocked and he challenges people constantly about who they are. He is absolute in the standard of behaviour he expects and he loves children dearly. He loves them so dearly that the Bible records how he scolded adults who stopped children coming to him – a reminder to all generations of how important children are to him. Jesus didn't seem bothered if those adults were offended by his public challenge – the children were paramount. And let's not forget those adults were Jesus' closest friends, but that didn't stop him reprimanding them and putting the children first.

The suffering Jesus endured on earth is a suffering he always knew about; it didn't catch him unawares because nothing catches him unawares. He knew he was fulfilling age-old prophecies when he died on the cross, and far from being out of control of his destiny, he showed unimaginable courage in accepting his cruel death for the love of human beings everywhere.

In terms of child protection it seems to me that churches are inordinately willing to display the character of Jesus described in paragraph two to the detriment of paragraph three. I see no place in the Bible where Jesus is (or calls for us to be) a sitting duck. His forgiveness and grace are magnificent beyond words – but they are not to be misused, and neither are we. Jesus tackled people, he was courageous, controversial and, at times, outspoken – often while delving into people's lives. I don't think it's wrong for us to be the same. For as long as some churches treat children's workers with an unquestioning acceptance, paedophiles will continue to treat churches as a hunting ground for children.

In the Child Protection Unit, I dealt with Mr H. He was the classic pillar-of-the-community type: a school governor, happily married with a few kids, and very involved in his local church. As part of an extended enquiry, his adult sister formally complained that Mr H had sexually abused her when she was a child. There was a big age gap between them, and he had been an adult for the years of the abuse. I arrested Mr H, and during a taped interview he admitted over a thousand rapes on his kid sister, along with other horrible acts of protracted abuse. The judge sent him to prison for five years (even though he was eligible for at least a thousand life sentences), and his church angrily rose up in his defence. Despite Mr H's full confession they maintained that he was innocent and that a serious miscarriage of justice was being upheld in sending him to prison. (The only miscarriage of justice I could see was the negligible length of time he was there!) The church used their funds to pay his mortgage while he was in prison and his family became heroes through martyrdom. Though well-meaning, the gullibility of that congregation was scary.

If my family joined your church next week and John asked to be treasurer I doubt that you would allow him. There'd be some hands on hips, some raised eyebrows, and mumblings to the tune of, 'But we don't know him. We can't let him loose with church funds. What audacity! The cheek of the man!' Quite right too; the very thought. We look after our money scrupulously and anyone who wants to be church treasurer has their credentials checked out for sure. Why don't we *all* do that for our children?

Throughout this chapter, I am going to expose what I believe are the main planks in a worrying fence that seems to encircle the church approach to protecting children. While all congregations would acknowledge that they couldn't love their kids any more if they tried (most of the time!), many struggle to enforce the relevant rules that place their safety at church before every other consideration. The fence obscures the clarity required for effective child protection – so let's take a look at the individual planks and hopefully tear down any fences that could be obscuring your church.

Note to any child protection co-ordinators: You did note my deliberate use of the word 'enforce', didn't you? The job you have at church is not a sweet and dandy one. Enforcing its responsibilities will sometimes set you against the tide and you will have to stand clear and firm – and maybe even alone – on occasions if you are to do your job properly. If you have a delicate constitution I advise you to resign now, or at least go off somewhere and develop the hide of a rhino as fast as you can. To enforce the protection of children effectively you're going to need it.

Some years ago, I was asked by my church leadership to create a child protection system for the church. It was to include a vetting process for children's workers, guidelines covering every scenario we could think of and a child protection policy that the membership would agree on. It is an understatement for me to say that if I had known then what I know now I would have suggested someone else for the job. The grief I have experienced through leading this area of the church has been manifold; it has been a thankless and isolating task – mainly because I have insisted on putting the kids first every time and few others seem to have grasped the consequences of that. A watertight child protection system at church always risks upsetting a few sensitive folk, but that has to be their problem because protection of the children is paramount.

Plank number 1

Most people advocate stringent child protection measures in society but they struggle with the principle of establishing them at church. The argument is that we shouldn't need them, God's house should be sacred, we might offend someone, we have to show Christ's grace and, anyway, we're all good eggs at church, we wouldn't do such a thing. This mentality is exactly why paedophiles target churches: the head-in-sand approach is an open invitation to them. Because the love of Jesus is such a protective love, church should be where kids are most protected, not most vulnerable. Because paedophiles target churches they are exactly the places where child protection systems should be the most stringent, *not* the most excusing. Churches must show the same resolve towards child protection that abusers show towards child abuse.

This is what happened in the first week of my new role as child protection co-ordinator for my church. A woman who was fairly new to the congregation was working among the teenagers and had been asked for her basic personal details. She had given her name and address but was refusing point-blank to reveal what her employment was. An assurance of confidentiality was given to her but she still refused. I came on board shortly afterwards – her refusal having been accepted – and said that the situation was unacceptable. She was expecting us to trust her with our most precious commodity (the children), and she was refusing to trust us with her employment details. They were relevant to who she was and besides, the longer her refusal went on the more suspicious I became and couldn't help wondering what she had to hide. I spoke to the woman and explained my concerns, leaving her with an ultimatum to either tell us what she did or – while remaining welcome at church – stand down from working with children. She maintained her stance and, within days, she had left the church. Her departure was regrettable and unnecessary, but the protection of the children was paramount.

At the same time I was told about a man who had recently joined the church and instantly got involved in the children's work. It seemed he didn't have a day to lose. Because he was so new, some Sunday school leaders asked for two references from previous churches which painted a conflicting picture of who he was. He had a complex church history in which he was the proverbial church-hopper, never staying in one congregation for very long and always getting involved with the kids' work within seconds of stepping through the door. You can imagine the clang of my alarm bells! He was asked to step down from children's work too, at least until I could delve deeper into who it was we were letting loose with the children. He left within days as well. His departure was regrettable and unnecessary, but the protection of the children was paramount.

Plank number 1 reminder

We have got to be this thorough and immovable with children's workers – I even checked out my own husband. He was a youth worker at the time I implemented the system, so it was only right that he submitted a comprehensive application form and referees just like anyone else. And in the interest of fairness, another church leader checked me out so that no one could complain I was the only one not going through the vetting mangle. No self-respecting children's worker will mind submitting to the process, and most will realize that it's as much about their own protection as the children's. The trauma of false accusation against adults is a growing process, and a stringently vetted worker is in a much stronger position to handle such an incident than an adult who is unchecked. You really are helping yourself – as individuals and as a body of people – if your system is rigorous and your workers co-operative. Child protection systems are a two-way street, and the more scrupulous the system, the more protection it offers everyone involved. If your church is cutting corners in this area you are heading for a crash; slack deployment of children's workers sends a powerful message to abusers and potential wolf-criers alike.

Let me say here: our church was a standard suburban church serving a standard suburban community. There was nothing unusual about it at all; it was as ordinary as your church. Don't read this chapter and dissociate yourself from its reality on the basis that your church is nicer, better, kinder, stronger, holier than ours. Believe me, what happened to us could happen to you. It might already have occurred or be taking place as you read. The biggest mistake you can make is to think these issues were our misfortune and could never be yours. Please, don't be as gullible as the paedophiles expect you to be!

Rather than jabber on about churches managing child protection, I want to talk you through the case of Mr I, which happened at our church. I dearly wish I could say this story is a fabrication, but I'm afraid every word is true. It deploys every plank I want to cover and builds the fence up for me. The story occurred shortly after another particularly nasty case – which constitutes Chapter 9 – and I had actually just stood down from leading the child protection because of the fallout from this saga. Suffice to say here that the men who dealt with Mr I assured me they had learnt their lessons from the disaster of Chapter 9. I'll leave you to make up your own mind on that one. In telling you about Mr I, I obviously draw on the failings of his case to highlight the pitfalls of churches managing paedophiles, so forgive me if this reads as a list of mistakes but the mistakes are the point of the story. Learning from them is a great form of education – and with Mr I, there were just so many of them!

The story of Mr I begins when he was arrested by the Police Paedophile Unit just a few months before I joined it. He still holds the dubious accolade of being the Unit's most deviant customer. We prefer that to 'school teacher' – he had worked a long career in both classroom and private tuition settings. His offending had continued undetected for thirty years, and his manipulation of people around him never let up, not even in custody where he tried to smooth-talk the coppers into disbelieving what they had just seen in his home with their own eyes. Mr I was released on police bail while his seized equipment was analysed, and he went straight home, I imagine, to think of a cunning plan. After all, he needed to extricate himself from the judicial hot water he found himself in before it boiled him alive (and now that the police had seized all his deviancy equipment, I suppose he didn't have much else to do with his time anyway). Hmm, a cunning plan, a cunning plan . . . it probably didn't burn too many of his brain cells to decide to join a local church and claim to be redeemed. That way, the judge would be thrilled with him, his sins appear forgiven, his character restored, and his freedom maintained. Oh, and through the church he would be able to find a way to carry on offending. I wouldn't be surprised if Mr I thought this very cunning plan would outwardly save his bacon and secretly feed his addiction. And I suspect he thought that no doubt the church people would play ball, because that's what church people do.

Within a week this middle-aged man was sitting at the front of our church as though he owned the place – having chosen not to be a churchgoer for most of his life. He tellingly sat among a section near the main doors where young families tended to sit because it gave them quick access to the toilets and crèche, etc. Everyone was supremely welcoming of this stranger and he was soon parked there with the regularity of a high fibre diet. He set about ingratiating himself with folk immediately, playing on his winsome 'teacher' employment (forgetting to say he'd been sacked for being a pervert), always full of smiles, conversation, and willing to help anyone. Let me tell you about his offences.

Mr I was obsessed with anything relating to toilets and backsides. Honestly, his video collection contained years of illicit footage of other people's youngsters in little gymslips and swimming costumes, always honing in on any occasions that the child bent down and accentuated their rear. He had done hours of secretive filming at school and hours from behind his bedroom curtain of children playing in the street. He loved kids' underpants, just a fleeting glance was enough, and his offending around toilets went into gruesome detail that I will spare you – but it included placing hidden cameras and tape recorders in cubicles to capture 'events' he could later replay for his pleasure. Can you imagine now what gratuitous fun Mr I must have had, sitting among those little ones at church every Sunday morning? Think of all the children who will have flashed their nappies and knickers to him . . . think of all the boys who used the toilets . . . think of all the opportunities he had to rig up cameras in there and check them every week. Church not only gave him an escape route from the consequences of his arrest, it gave him an arena in which to continue offending. Ain't church great! What other facility in the community could tick all those boxes? And so naively too.

The church adults were easily groomed. Mr I played on his loneliness, omitting to say he didn't have any friends left because he had abused their children. Once the compassion of a select few at church had been cultivated deeply enough, including leaders, he confided in them about the judicial hot water he was in. He thought such honesty would win him massive brownie points and it did – because he cooled the temperature of the water and didn't confide the truth. He wasn't daft, he was devious – all paedophiles are. He admitted that he was going to court soon about child-related offences, but he was not truthful about their detail. Unfortunately for him I had a foot in both of his worlds shortly after his trial – I knew nothing about him up until then – and when I compared the police account to the church account there was little correlation.

Throughout the months of the previous child protection nightmare I kept telling the church leadership that paedophiles are devious, manipulative, we've got to be careful, they rarely rehabilitate, they are not to be trusted. Despite these warnings the leadership were taken in by Mr I and offered him their support.

Plank number 2

Supporting paedophiles is not wrong, but *unquestioning* support of them is *dangerously* wrong. Jesus helps paedophiles – but not blindly. He brings their behaviour into the glare of his light, and we must do the same. Paedophiles are devious and in control: if churches accept the things they say without rigorously testing them, churches will be full of paedophiles. It's as simple as that.

I know of another church that did not have any child protection system in place; they relied on knowing and trusting each other as a much kinder way to go about it. Then the Boys' Brigade Captain happened to change his employment and apply for a position within the Education Department who discovered that he had previous convictions for sexual offences against young boys. With nothing in place, the church struggled to evict him from his BB post within their deep commitment to supporting him – and then he went on to join the Sunday school. The protection of children in that church was dangerously compromised through a commitment to blindly supporting the paedophile ahead of acting firmly on the blatantly obvious risk he presented.

The accepting support Mr I was offered by our church was a big problem, but thanks to a local newspaper it didn't last too long. One Saturday morning, John came home from his weekly jaunt to the paper shop and slapped the local rag down on the kitchen counter. A full-page mugshot of Mr I glowered back at me as John wailed, 'It's him! It's that bloke from church who sits at the front with the kids.' Then we learned from the newspaper about how he had been convicted of his years of offending at Crown Court and sent to prison for a few months. (Sorry to labour the point, but did you spot the dismal comparison between the '*years* of offending' and 'sent to prison for a few *months*'?) Of course Mr I had exaggerated his church credentials before the judge to help his cause and, before the first echo of his slamming prison door, he was smooth-talking the church leadership about his return to the congregation when he was released. The prospect of coming back to church seemed to be the way he coped with imprisonment (though he could have blinked to miss the sentence), and he maintained his grooming of those adults from inside. The people in contact with him thought this was an encouraging sign of his spiritual growth – I thought it was an alarming sign of his enjoyment of our children.

There's a postscript here that hammers plank 1 securely to this story: some of the church leadership had known for months that Mr I was awaiting trial for child-related offences, yet they had watched him deliberately sit among young families every week when there were plenty of other seats elsewhere he could have warmed. Why didn't they identify that as a concern and require him to sit away from the children? I presume they didn't want to cause offence, they wanted to offer a welcome, they wanted to trust him, they were sure it would be fine. *No, it wasn't fine*. It was a preventable failure of those families, and a particular failure of those children whose bodies and underwear he enjoyed such close proximity to for months. Requiring him to sit elsewhere would have told Mr I that we were a church who were not sitting ducks and not afraid to address him. It would have told him that our children were paramount. But instead they left him to it, and – despite a child protection policy being in place to claim otherwise – the children weren't paramount. No one wanted to offend Mr I.

Plank number 3

I believe the gospel message is misunderstood when it comes to child protection. The unconditional nature of Jesus' love can actually go against children by leaving churches feeling compelled to treat paedophiles unconditionally. It's a tragedy and ripe to be exploited. Paedophiles can be part of church life only under stringent conditions – I don't believe Jesus expects them to be let loose among children and neither should we. His love does not condone placing children in danger, just as it does not condone rejecting Mr I. It is big enough to keep children safe and place proper boundaries around Mr I designed to respect everyone, including him. Remember: every paedophile is a potentially hungry tiger prowling round your congregation. Do not leave him untethered or unaddressed; under those conditions he will maul your children. Upset him if you have to, but enforce rigorous boundaries to protect your children before all other considerations. Zoos don't let tigers prowl about – they care for them within protective parameters. It's much the same thing.

While Mr I was in prison, I entered into discussions with the church leadership about him, especially as he was fixed on returning to the congregation as soon as his release allowed. I was horrified to hear how weakly he had been treated so far, and was as determined that he shouldn't return to the church untethered, as he was determined to come back. Some of the leaders had been present at court, which was helpful – they had learned the full truth about the deviancy of his offending and the level of risk he presented. They also accepted that he was so entrenched in his addiction he was showing no remorse and completely failing to understand what everyone was so concerned about. His offending had become 'normal' to him over the years and our fears seemed only to bemuse him. The church leadership remained committed to meeting Mr I's spiritual needs – and I honour them for that – but the children of the church had to come first in considering how to do this. It was imperative that extensive boundaries were placed around him and rigorously enforced, the difficulty being that any plans had to cover the fact that he was obsessed with toilets. That meant that any church activity with lavatory facilities was one he couldn't attend. Well, where there are people there are lavatories, so that left our options somewhat caught short – so to speak.

A week later I received a triumphant call from one of the leaders – they'd solved it! Mr I would be told he couldn't come to church on a Sunday but he could join a house group that met in private homes during the week. My initial hope that a solution had been found was dashed quicker than Mr I might say 'Andrex'. I took no pleasure in reminding the leader that there were children in all the homes holding house groups (and even if there weren't, the poor souls who hosted the group would have their bathroom bugged for sure). Far from solving anything, the plan played right into Mr I's hands by furnishing him with plentiful opportunities to offend. It also probably reminded him of why he chose a church for his cunning plan – they would be so keen to accommodate him they would overlook the full picture, even when they knew how very full it was.

Plank number 4

Think laterally! Paedophiles are innately resourceful; it's part of being devious. You must think outside of the box in any dealings you have with them, plan as laterally as possible when you consider behavioural boundaries or prepare anything relating to child protection. Tear holes in every solution you come up with until it is hole-proof. Do not be fooled, especially by solutions that offenders themselves suggest. It may appear practicable to you, but they will have suggested it for a reason and there will be an opportunity for offending built into it somewhere. The house group idea was never going to be a safe option regarding Mr I – and it worried me that those in leadership thought it was.

The day of Mr I's release arrived all too soon and he was given an absolute warning that he was not to return to the church on a Sunday morning or enter the building at any other time. We weren't being harsh on him, we were protecting our children. A group of people were tipped off to watch the door and ensure he didn't come in – we had to be more determined than he was. The leadership offered him personal meetings at the church when no other people were present and arranged that a group of at least three men would meet with him and offer spiritual guidance if he was still committed to learning about the Christian faith. This was a good and generous solution and I have to say I credit those men for devising this way forward. It offered him genuine help for as long as he required it, and it upheld the protection of children as paramount. (I never actually asked any of them, but I guess the men involved didn't drink anything for a good few hours before the meetings as none of them would have wanted to visit the gents with Mr I around. When paedophiles get close and personal, it's amazing how people change their stance.)

I did shoot one warning across the bows of this excellent solution: my concern was that Mr I would say and do all the right things at their meetings, then at some calculated point claim to be redeemed. Then he could demand to be allowed back among the congregation to offend. My gut instinct was that this was his sole motivation for agreeing to the meetings. Such a claim on his part would leave the church men in a difficult position, and it was one they should be aware of from the outset. The leader I spoke to was shocked by my 'cynicism', and we had to end our conversation with a difference of opinion: he was encouraged by Mr I's commitment to spiritual growth and I was worried Mr I was abusing their good natures to serve his deviancy. The group meeting with him consisted of professional men who had child protection training coming out of their ears, and it was on the basis of this training that I was told not to worry. Things went quiet for a while – commonly known as the lull before the storm.

Plank number 5

Many Christians have a deep desire to believe the best in people, certainly until proven otherwise. With paedophiles, you have to work in the opposite direction. If churches are to robustly protect their children, paedophiles must be doubted and questioned until there is no doubt and there are no more questions – not the other way around. It's not a pleasant way to operate, especially within the ethos of church and Christian values – but paedophiles themselves are not functioning within that ethos and we have to be one step ahead. However much it goes against the grain, we must doubt and question, doubt and question; the abuse of a child goes more against the grain than doubting and questioning adults. If you can keep that principle at the forefront of your thinking then the doubts and questions become more palatable. Do you want to know what happened next with Mr I?

By now I was working in the Paedophile Unit and a close colleague was aware that I was attending the same church that was helping him. (By the way, my colleagues were staggered by how much value the church placed by Mr I's rights to spiritual help compared to how little value they had placed by the children's rights to be safe at church. Not a good witness at all.) My close colleague spoke to me one morning and wanted to discuss one of the church men, who was meeting regularly with Mr I. I sensed by her question that trouble was on the agenda and was shaking my head in my hands as she explained: Mr I had persuaded this man to complete a job reference for him enabling him to work in a local charity shop. The man's reference described Mr I as 'trustworthy' and recommended him for the job; he did not give the slightest hint that Mr I was banned from the church for being a highly dangerous and non-trustworthy sex offender. Within half an hour, my colleague and I were on the doorstep of this man seeking an explanation.

His starting place was that he had just wanted to help the poor bloke, give him a second chance, offer him some respect, show graciousness and compassion. He said that Mr I told him he was desperate to work for something constructive to do and to contribute back to society something for what he had taken from it. Mr I had also implied that he would be working during the week among other adult volunteers and, as such, it was the ideal job for him. Trying not to sound too incredulous, we asked why the man had described Mr I as 'trustworthy' when he was one of the dodgiest characters in town. He gloomily explained he had meant 'trustworthy' in terms of money and not thought beyond any the other connotations of the word. Then my colleague dropped her bomb.

Mr I had been frequenting the charity shop for weeks, grooming the staff. On a Saturday morning, a young teenage girl helped out behind the counter. Far from wanting to work there during the week, he had actually applied to only work on Saturday mornings, apparently to gain access to the girl. Now that the church door had shut in his face, he had to find yet another avenue for offending and this was obviously his latest cunning plan. The charity shop had one communal toilet at the back for employees to use – perfect. And the church people did exactly what I suspect he always knew they would do: even when armed with the truth about him, they just wanted to help and were guided by that above everything else.

In the job application Mr I lied about his previous convictions, he lied about being sacked from teaching for being a sex offender, and he drew immense credibility from the reference of a respected church member saying he was a trustworthy character just wanting to help the community.

Finally, the penny dropped for this member. Its resounding crash into his thinking was painful to watch as he realized that he had been completely fooled by Mr I, despite my strong warnings. His good nature had overridden what he knew was good practice – and he was a professional person full to the brim with child protection training. Worse still, his foolishness had become a significant pawn in Mr I's apparent plan to abuse a teenage girl. We left him in great distress and both felt really sorry for him.

Plank number 6

Do not be led by conscience when dealing with paedophiles in church – be led by the fact that the protection of children is paramount. Your feelings are irrelevant. Your responsibilities must override them. Yes, paedophiles have a right to find Christ, of course they do and I utterly concur with that. Their right to faith is not diminished by the enforcement of protective parameters, but a child's right to safety is gravely reduced when conscience blurs the strong clarity required to deal with the devious ways of sex offenders. After this incident, Mr I was finally asked to leave the church. It was recognized that he did not wish to search for God but was seemingly committed only to abusing our children and misusing our trust. After he had gone, one leader spoke to me with deep concern about how he would cope if the church's dismissal of Mr I drove him to suicide. With due respect to this man, his concern was not about Mr I and definitely not about the children, it was about the placating of his own conscience. I understand that features for all of us – in different measure – but it can't dictate how we protect children.

The last I heard of Mr I was when a friend told me she had overheard him talking in a local café months later. He was telling the proprietor that he was a teacher and was heavily involved with our church, and then he offered to help the proprietor's children with private tuition. I passed her report to the detective responsible for his management under the Sex Offenders Register.

During the time of Mr I, and indeed the Chapter 9 story, our church had robust child protection systems in place. Every children's worker and youth worker had to complete a detailed seven-page application form that asked intrusive questions about health, employment, and any legal/Social Services involvement, along with two personal references, Christian testimony, family circumstances, history of working with children, and shoe size. (Only joking about the shoes.) It then required workers to undergo a Criminal Records Bureau check to establish any relevant criminal convictions. Running parallel to this was a detailed child protection policy to be ratified at a church members' meeting and a number of guidelines covering subjects from children who disclose abuse to caring for youngsters requiring help in the bathroom. So why didn't the system work? Surely such a robust system should have prevented the disasters that beset us.

A good child protection system is only as good as the resolve of the people responsible for it. We could have had a system so good it detected sex offenders a hundred yards off by the colour of their vest but, for as long as the leaders struggled to enforce its requirements and failed to resist the planks, it would not be much use. Your church system will work if you enforce it – otherwise it won't. At the close of this book I have outlined the system we had in place covering these processes in more detail.

Plank number 7

I've saved the worst plank till last: 'Sit back and hope nothing happens.' *This is not the way to protect children*. It fills me with despair when I hear how many churches are relying on this reckless method instead of establishing a proper system of child protection. Plank number 7 is about apathy and denial, and it's the least excusable to me. It's like not bothering with the Highway Code in the hope that you won't get knocked down anyway – none of us do that!

One weekend, a group of church teenagers went away for an outward bound course. On the night before they left, I was rung at home and asked for a copy of the child protection policy to take with them, should they need it. I stalled for two reasons which I won't bore you with now. This stall was not appreciated, and in the ensuing discussion the person concerned said the horrifying words, 'I don't know what you're so worried about, nothing's going to happen anyway.' *I beg you not to run your church's child protection on this basis.* Anything can happen anywhere to anyone at any time and churches must be ready, must be rigorous and must be resolute that the protection of children is paramount.

The flip side

There is a sad flip side to the child protection coin at church. Of course the overwhelming majority of churchgoers are good, honest people of God who abhor the abuse of children. The confusion and sensitivity that surrounds child protection can inadvertently cause people, especially men, to walk on eggshells when youngsters are around. They daren't go near a child for fear of being suspected of terrible things, let alone volunteer to teach Sunday school. But children need the men to love them just as demonstratively as the women, and child protection systems don't have to affect that. A good set of guidelines marks out sensible practices that anyone other than a pervert is living by anyway. Child protection is not about crippling church life with neuroticism or suspicion; it is actually about creating the opposite ethos. A good and visible system tells everyone to relax. The subject is covered, the youngsters are paramount and we all know what is expected of us. Parents relax in the knowledge that their children are in the best possible care and adults can interact with children knowing they are free to be themselves if their motives are right. With a good system, it's only if you are a paedophile looking to cross the line that you need to walk on eggshells.

A few years back, a single man at our church had a quiet word in my ear. This cracking guy is one of life's hard workers and absolutely fantastic with the kids. He confided his deep concern that being single made him self-conscious that people would question the strength of his relationships with youngsters. *His* presumption was that *their* presumption equated 'single-man-around-children' to 'pervert'. This next sentence is for every single man who loves the company of children for all the right reasons: I told this guy that in the Unit I deal with far more attached men than single ones. The relief that flooded his face tugged my heartstrings, and I was glad to watch, over the months, that his rare gift with children did not wane through fear of misunderstanding.

Fundamental parameters

There are a few fundamental parameters for all of us regarding our children at church. They're basic but they're important.

Physical contact

Physical contact is always on the child's terms and for their benefit – not the adult's. It's a simple rule that we can all uphold. It doesn't mean we can't instigate physical contact – it means that it must always be for the child's sake and with their total agreement. Yes, there are obvious exceptions like administering medical treatment, and the rare highly sexualized child, but let's not get entangled with those.

When our youngest girl was four years old, I watched her hurtle into the church hall and spot a man who is a close family friend. She charged at him in delight, at great speed and I watched to see what would happen – willing him to return her enthusiasm. He did. He scooped her up in the bear hug she was anticipating, swung her round, and set her down on her feet again. She was happy with that, and toddled off to accost his wife whose tights were begging to be laddered. What he did was absolutely right. The physical contact they shared was on her terms, for her benefit and he matched her excitement without exploiting it. She trusted him, and he did not fail that trust on any level; they were in a public place and, as families, we had a strong friendship. But the other way around . . . oh, no! If he had rushed across the room and sought her out for cuddles I would have flattened him with a well-thrown hymn book. And I guess in private too he would have been wise to have responded to her with a bit more distance – though she would have still deserved a welcoming response.

The issue of physical contact is always going to be a very subjective one, because it is highly personal and individual. If our daughters are upset at church, there are some folk that I would expect to cuddle them and would be distressed if they didn't. There are other folk that I wouldn't expect to touch them on the grounds that they're strangers to us and not in a position to be so familiar. We all know our relationships with individual children, their families, and our own personalities regarding how demonstrative we naturally are. Crucially, we also know each other on that basis too, and will notice someone behaving outside of accepted social boundaries in terms of hugging and cuddling children. If you're alone with a child, then I recommend you avoid physical contact as much as you can, though that is not always appropriate and again very dependent on both the child and adult involved and the relationship they share. A friend recently had an incident at their youth group where a teenage girl was distressed at the close of the meeting and asked to confide in a male leader who she knew well. For privacy, they stood down the side of the church to talk, and she has since accused him of being inappropriate with her.

Accountability

The root of a healthy church environment is accountability. If individuals are accountable to God in a true way, and then accountable to each other, the church is free to function fully and without fear: the boundaries of accountability bring freedom, not trouble. That principle is also the root of healthy child protection within a church. It is right to raise concerns when you have them. With every child protection case I have dealt with there has always been an individual in the background who has had concerns about the child and not felt able to raise them. Fears of being nosey, wrong, over-sensitive, or even ridiculed quash the nagging concern that something is not quite right. Choosing who you confide in is as important as choosing to confide – but it is imperative that concerns are shared, not dismissed. A child's life may depend on it. With the tragic death of Victoria Climbié that was literally the case. If you have concerns about a child you must raise them. You are accountable to that little one, to your Lord and to your own integrity far more than to the adult in question. Child protection systems hold us all accountable on every level – for our own actions, for the safety of children, and for each other. I think these systems liberate adults to enjoy children as they should, secure in the knowledge that the boundaries for effective interaction are in place to bind everyone together in accountability, not divide them with suspicion.

To conclude: Church child protection systems are no different to church fire regulations – and I've never come across a church member who disputes having those. Congregations accept that the outbreak of fire is a terrifying experience and, though it is highly unlikely, it is still one we must guard against. Regulations are drawn up and fulfilled, even if they are inconvenient, state the obvious, and upset somebody. Of course the regulations don't guarantee there won't be a fire, but they do offer good practice and common sense towards its prevention and containment. Fire exits, fire drills, fire alarms, fire policies – they all bring a peace of mind to our behaviour at church. We know the subject is covered and we can relax. Even when there hasn't been a fire for thirty years we still don't question the necessity of abiding by the regulations – we can't take any chances. Most of us would behave as the regulations dictate anyway, only an arsonist would traverse them, but we don't mind the guidelines being in place and they don't change our behaviour. Knowing there are fire regulations does not make me nervous about using the church kettle! We examine our church buildings, we doubt and question and then we strengthen any weak spots we identify. Lazy denial regarding an outbreak of fire is not an option, and anyone suspected of contravening the regulations is dealt with robustly. Special events like barbecues and candlelit carol services have special fire measures applied – there is a greater risk on those occasions and we are meticulous about being more careful.

Please don't question the need for your church to have a robust child protection system that is rigorously enforced. You do everything to save yourself from fire – do everything to save your children from abuse.

You couldn't make it up

As you may have gathered, running the child protection of my church was not a heart-warming experience, but thankfully God is supremely gracious and he provided me with a few chinks of humour along the way. Instigating the system was a massive administrative task, and required me to read over ninety application forms and 180 references about people in the church. A tight rein of confidentiality was placed on me in respect of this – fair enough – but reading the various entries that people submitted was a source of great amusement and it would be a travesty not to be able to share some of the clangers.

For example, under the section on criminal convictions I was amused to see how many church members confessed to speeding fines. A speeding fine is not a criminal conviction, so they didn't need to confess them, but so many people coughed to having them I wondered whether I should be giving motoring advice during the training evenings rather than child protection. I'm not sure what caused the epidemic, but

I did suggest the church bought bus passes in bulk because lots of folk looked likely to need them. (Unfortunately I must now count myself among their number having twice set off the same local speed camera in twenty-four hours. An expensive business!)

On the application form, two referees were required for each applicant and most people used only other church members for this. We quickly changed the rules to require that at least one referee was from outside the church; the system was becoming too insular which threatened its integrity. However, this was not before one member had volunteered their best friend to write a reference for them – and in the course of the reference the best friend described them as 'very irritating'. Oh the fun I could have had with that little gem.

The best application entry came from a married person. They had put down their spouse as a referee (which was as unorthodox as it was unacceptable). Then in answer to the question that asked, 'In what capacity do you know this referee?' the applicant had written, 'family friend'. Seeing as they had children, that was quite a relief. But it made us wonder what kind of friendships they indulged in and we decided that we're never going there for Sunday lunch.

5.

'How Do You Do Your Job?'

If I had a pound for every time I have been asked, 'How do you do your job?' I doubt I would be sitting here writing about it. I'd be agonizing over which beach-front mansion to stay in this weekend and which vintage champagne Jeeves should have waiting in the ice bucket. And why choose Jeeves anyway? Why not one of my other butlers!

In policing the world of indecent images I do a job that is as revolting as it is fascinating, as isolating to people as it is compelling for them, as commented-on as it is a mystery. Most people have an opinion on my job, but how I actually cope with the gruesome reality of what I see is often where their opinions end and the questions begin. I guess people ask me how I do my job in much the same way I would ask a pathologist – with morbid intrigue that wants to know the answer but doubts I will understand it.

Last year we travelled as a family to my husband's old church about a hundred miles away from our home town. We hadn't been to the church for ages and took the impetuous decision to drive down, as much out of curiosity as anything: does so-and-so still go there, and so on. The church service itself was great, and afterwards we engaged in a few conversations with people who all remembered John but couldn't remember me. (I am still trying to work out if there's a way I can take that as a compliment.) One couple, though, will never forget me after that visit, I am sure.

John and I were walking out to the car park with this pair and having one of those polite chats in which everyone was showing interest in the answers but were pretty much guaranteed to have forgotten what was said by dinnertime.

When the couple asked John what I do for a living he quietly answered, 'She watches porn.' Then he fell silent and left that remark fizzing in mid-air. The poor souls turned an ashen shade of dead as they desperately searched for a suitable response: 'Oooh, yes, so do I'/'How interesting, tell me more'/'But your wife looks like such a nice girl'. What *could* they say? John soon put us all out of our misery with an explanation. But it clearly horrified them even more to think that I viewed indecent images of children for a living.

You are now either chuckling at my husband's (warped) sense of humour, or you are affronted by the playing of such a mean and uncouth trick on perfectly decent people. Such contrary responses are the instincts this subject evokes, and in this chapter more than any other I can only tell you how it is for me. (I thought John was hilarious.) You may sympathize with me in these pages or you may be outraged, but please bear with me.

A Christian . . .

The bedrock of my life is that I am a Christian. My faith is me, and everything else that defines me originates from my implacable belief in Jesus Christ as God's Son and Saviour of the world. There are many misunderstandings about the Christian faith, but the expected purity of those who follow it is not often one of them. The Bible is emphatic about the standards of behaviour God requires for his creation, and watching pornography does not fall into these edicts – yet I watch pornography a lot. Occasionally mainstream adult images, often extremely depraved adult images, and frequently the abusive defilement of children. My testimony is that my job has never conflicted with my faith in God – in fact the complete opposite is true. It is my faith that enables me to go to work.

Child abuse is arguably one of the murkiest worlds on the planet, and it usually leaves me feeling as though my mind is in a swamp. Imagine sticking your head down a drain and pulling it out again to find oodles of long dank gunk clinging to your ears. Wading through indecent images of children is like drain-dunking your brain. During a viewing session I often have to take time out and leave the room for a blast of fresh air, or engage in conversation with a colleague about the price of fresh tomatoes these days; anything at all to resurface from the inevitable sinking feeling. That lead weight of foulness gets heavier and heavier in your consciousness with every image you see, with every scream you hear.

But I believe in a God who is always, *always* greater than the worst evil, and it is the strength of this belief that keeps me from drowning in the swamp.

Without exception I pray in the car on the way to work; it is not a mantra or a ritual, it is the way I prepare my mind for the day ahead, just as in getting dressed I prepare my body. In the Bible, the apostle Paul encourages believers to find their strength through God instead of relying on their own capabilities. He outlines how to do that by portraying God's help as a spiritual suit of armour we can put on. And so, every morning on the way to work, I pray through each piece of armour Paul describes in Ephesians 6:13–17, asking God to strengthen me for the day ahead. He has never, ever failed to do so. God always shows up when we ask him to, and I know that with his help I 'see' the images, but I do not 'absorb' them. I believe that God keeps them from sinking into my psyche and inhabiting my memory. Yes, they trouble me at work when I watch them, but I never store them in my head for them to trouble me at home. I believe that the principle of God's armour does exactly what it says on the tin (well, in the Book); it protects me from taking the mental and emotional blows that pornographic material is capable of inflicting upon me.

There is a huge difference between not being troubled at home and becoming desensitized. From my years in the Child Protection Unit I learned that to work in this area I had to locate the thin but life-saving line between not becoming so emotionally involved that I went to pieces and not hardening up so much that I lost sight of the subject's awfulness. You cannot be effective if you crack up but equally, you cannot be effective if you harden. *My faith is my line.* I care deeply for the poor innocents who I see suffering and my faith is the channel for that deep human reaction, filtering the horror away from my consciousness and into God's enormity. It doesn't stop the horror from arriving in the first place though, and I wouldn't want it to. The day I desensitize to child abuse is the day I have the biggest problem of all. Many is the time I have slapped the lap-top lid down in distress, unable to watch another image; many is the time I have prayed to God for the poor kid whose rape I am watching with clenched hands and tearful eyes. As with my colleagues, my pain breeds a steely determination to catch every monster I can who enjoys these crimes, and

voices gratitude to God for his help in draining away the
filth and leaving me with this resolve.

A while ago, John and I were watching a film set in
the Wild West of America which followed the journey of
a white city-type man across the plains. At one point he
was helped by a group of Indian settlers who bravely
crossed the race divide to offer him some assistance. He
became one of their group, and later had the devastating
experience of watching the Indians massacred by a
posse of violent cowboys. The massacre scene was not
particularly graphic, but I couldn't bear to watch. I had
to turn my head away from the horror of it and ask John
to tell me when it was over.

He laughed, 'But Rebecca, you watch far worse than
this at work – and that stuff's real, this is just a film.'

Then it hit me how extensively God puts up a protective barrier for me at work that is not necessary at home.
I can self-police what I watch at home; it is at work that
I need his defence. The impact that the revolting side of
my job can have on me is one I believe he absorbs on my
behalf – if God did not protect me at work I do not think
I could watch the images at all. If he was leaving me to
watch them in my own strength I would have been able
to watch that film. God places a value on children that
humankind cannot emulate, and in doing a job that
seeks to protect them and bring their abusers to justice, I
am confident I am doing a job he approves of.

. . . a wife and a mother . . .

After first defining myself as a Christian, I define myself
as a wife and a mother. John is also a police officer and
we have been married for eleven years – to him it probably feels like eleven decades. He is innately patient

with his feisty wife, and if I had to go to the ends of the earth to snatch a moment with him I would crawl there on my hands and knees. (But don't tell him I said so; I'm chipping away at him to get me a new washing machine and such devotion may not help my cause.) Our two daughters are growing up far too fast, and we think they're the best kids ever.

Soon after I started in the Unit, John and I were prompted to reach an agreement about how much I talk about the images at home; no limit on discussing the other aspects of my job, but definite boundaries on airing the images. We agreed that if I felt sufficiently upset by one then it would be healthy for me to come home and describe it to him so that he could support me. But once shared and consoled, it should be forgotten. If I was still dwelling on the image hours later and showing obvious signs of distress then that was an indication that I was no longer coping and we would review my employment. Neither of us was prepared to ignore any warning signs to the detriment of my well-being. We consider that my well-being sets the tone for the girls' well-being and they have always come before my career. Thanks to the protective barrier God has kept around me, our agreement is not often required and has never been breached. The fact that John is a highly experienced copper who has seen the worst side of life for twenty years does not alter his revulsion at the images I describe to him. By his facial expression you would think I was frying his eyeballs; right-minded people are repulsed by child abuse. I do not buy the theory that there is a grey area to that. If you are not repulsed by child abuse you have a serious problem.

One of the unexpected missiles the job has fired at me is distress caused by something comparatively innocuous in an image. You steel yourself for the graphic depictions of children suffering, you know they're going to be tough to watch, but I have found it is often that relatively nondescript little something that has struck me in the gut. The first time it happened I was caught completely off-guard, and it was this particular image that provoked John's and my agreement. I was prepared for some horrid stuff and watching a series of nasty images depicting young children in violent sexual scenarios. I was doing OK as the images rolled on, conscious of God's barrier and fulfilling the professional tasks that mean I have to view the material at all.

Then up flashed a picture of a little boy being hit within a sexual setting – it was no different in severity to any of the other pictures I was viewing. The boy was about five years of age and he was being beaten by an adult – the photo of this violence was graphic, but it wasn't this explicitness that got me, it was his little hand. Down in the bottom left corner of the photo I saw his hand clenched tightly round some furniture. He was gripping the wood so desperately his knuckles were white from the intensity, and that little hand told me everything. It said how much it was hurting and how frantically he was trying to bear the pain. It said he was helpless and unable to take any better measures to protect himself. His hand broke my heart, and is probably the image I remember most keenly. I can't entirely explain why that is so, as I have seen far worse – indeed his own beating was nasty enough – but that little hand was crying out for a rescue I could not effect. I realized that in trying to help these kids I was helpless myself; perhaps it was that stark and unpleasant realization that triggered such a strong reaction.

I have never personalized my job to my family. When I see indecent images of girls my daughters' age I don't envisage my children, and when I see my daughters I don't think of the images. I couldn't continue in the job if I did. The children in the images are unrelated to my children and that distinction has never become blurred. To be honest, I think my girls actually help me to leave my work at work, because as soon as I finish in the office I am off to collect them from school and a rapid transition is forced upon me. I am catapulted into the harmless chaos of the playground as two excited faces run nearer and nearer towards me, until bang! Their bodies hurtle into me as they shove their school bags into my hands – since when was I the family carthorse? – and then the verbal diarrhoea begins, destined not to fall silent until bedtime. 'Jane pushed me at lunchtime . . . I'm on reading book seven now, Mummy . . . Can Danny come to tea? Ohhhhh, why not? It's not fair, you always say that.' The images are instantly forgotten and my 'mummy' hat takes precedence over my 'policewoman' one.

I suspect I parent my children slightly differently because of my job to how I would if I did not have this exposure to paedophiles. It is obviously every parent's worst nightmare that their child should fall into the hands of a monster and I do not claim a monopoly on that fear – but I do have an obsessive edge to my parenting that is hard to keep in check. Paedophiles are at the forefront of my maternal mind. Literally this morning I was having coffee with a friend in Starbucks when she told me about her seven-year-old daughter who had become bored at a large social event and began doing handstands.

'You know what kids are like, Rebecca. She was just doing these handstands everywhere and I kept thinking she'll kick someone, or knock something over, or end up hurting herself.'

All *I* could think was, 'I hope she didn't flash her knickers at anyone.' The rest of my friend's concerns would not have featured in my mind until long after that one.

Maybe I'm fortunate to be this aware or maybe I really am obsessive, but as long as my kids reach adulthood unscathed, to tell you the truth I'm not too bothered.

Take Brownie camp for example.

A few months ago my eldest daughter joyfully brought home a letter announcing that the Brownies were going away for a weekend camp. My face fell to my boots with the same vigour that her face was brightly shining and I scanned the letter nervously while I thought to myself, 'You have absolutely no chance of going on this camp in a month of Sundays, darling.' She was oblivious to my reaction, and already planning which pyjamas she was going to pack and which vests she was definitely not going to pack. Reading the letter did not assuage my fears at all. No mention was made of any child protection matters and no detail was given of the staff that would be present apart from Brown Owl herself. I wasn't interested in the paragraphs of activities they would undertake and meals they would have; the fire regulations featured (fair enough) and even catering for children with dietary needs. But there was *nothing* about child protection. That was all I wanted to know about. 'Who is going to look after her? Who is going to put her to bed? Who will be there during the night? Will there be any men around? Have they been checked out? How secure is the camp?' I couldn't understand that a whole paragraph had been dedicated to the singular child on a vegetarian diet and not a word had been written about the protection of the whole group. I made my excuses to Brown Owl and my daughter was the one of the tiny minority who did not go on the camp. I couldn't trust it.

I don't want to blight her life – I settle my own conscience by organizing alternative events to compensate –

but I could not release my daughter into the care of unidentified strangers for a weekend. To my mind, the risks involved in that could blight her life far more catastrophically than missing one Brownie camp. You may be wondering why I didn't just ask Brown Owl the questions I wanted answers to. Well, I reasoned that if the paramount issues were not important enough to merit a fleeting reference in the letter, then I could not rely on them *being* paramount – whatever assurances she gave me. That either makes me neurotic, cynical or very careful. And seeing as my children are my most precious treasure, I like to be *very* careful indeed.

A month later, a similar scenario arose.

This time the Brownies were going bowling (I've got nothing against Brownies by the way!) and we had to drop the children at the normal meeting hall for them to be transported in other people's cars to the bowling alley. I must have been a few minutes late, because when I arrived at the hall most of the girls had left and there was just one car waiting to transport the remnants. Brown Owl abruptly told me that there was one place left in a car – and frogmarched my daughter into the back seat of a car being driven by a man I have never clapped eyes on before. His own daughters were in the car too – but oh, the agony of letting her drive off with that man! I wrestled with it like crazy, especially when I saw the pleading look on my daughter's face that was saying, 'Don't make a fuss, Mum! Please don't make a fuss, just this once.' Against every instinct in me, I allowed her to be driven away to the bowling alley in that car – and I regret it to his day. I had noted his number plate and a full description of him and his vehicle, I had trusted him because of the strong friendship he clearly had with Brown Owl – and my daughter had a fantastic time bowling – but I still bitterly regret what I did. I should have driven her there myself and never permitted her to go with a stranger like that. I will never do it again.

And then there are sleepovers – perishing sleepovers. I'm sure I can't be the only parent who would love to call an amnesty on them; to me they are more worry than they're worth. The thing with sleepovers is that nagging fear that you never really know for sure. You might be well acquainted with the mum and think she's great, but do you know the dad? Do you know the uncle who pops in for a beer during the evening and keeps nipping upstairs to the loo or the neighbour who comes round to borrow a spanner and overstays his welcome? I do allow my children to go for the occasional sleepover – but only when I know, when I *really* know, for sure. And just when you think you've got the sleepover issue sorted, there are babysitters to get your head around . . .

Our wider family live a fair distance away from us and so do not make viable babysitters. Identifying someone who does has not been easy – most of our friends have their own kids to take care of and we're too stingy to pay some teenagers a greater amount of money than we would spend on ourselves while we were out. When our youngest daughter was a toddler we hit the jackpot and struck a great deal with some close friends who did not have little children of their own. They both worked full-time, so the agreement was that I left a meal for them in our oven, and they sat in our house and ate it after a long day at the office, so we could go out. The deal scratched both our backs and worked a treat for some years. The aside to this deal was that the husband was a senior police officer and the wife a specialist medic. Babysitters don't come with better credentials than that – and the kids reliably tell me that they were great story-tellers too. Last Christmas they recounted how she told the story and he contributed the 'Ho Ho Ho'. If only the Home Office could have heard him.

The husband never babysat alone. It's not that we didn't trust him with our children – he knew our trust in him was implicit – it's that most importantly, *he wouldn't have wanted to*, and we wouldn't have wished it *on him*. The awkward position it would have placed him in would have been unfair: if one of the girls had wet the bed or been seeking undue affection, he would have felt extremely uncomfortable dealing with them alone. The children loved him to bits and trusted him as we did – but for the benefit of everyone we would never have expected him to do something so potentially compromising. I risk being shot down in flames for this next sentence, but can only be honest in saying I would question any man who was pushing to babysit my kids on his own. I'm not saying it makes him a paedophile, I'm saying I would question his keenness and the risky position it placed everyone in. Ultimately, I'd rather be wrong and upset the bloke than be right and watch my daughters live with the consequences. Babysitting is the classic domain of the child sex offender and, although playing safe may render me neurotic, at least the kids are safe.

A parental quandary arose for us when I moved into the Paedophile Unit from mainstream uniformed policing. When I had left the house for work in my white shirt and black trousers the children could readily accept that Mummy went to work to be a police lady where she caught all the burglars and banged them up in jail. (If only.) Consequently it came as a shock to them when I started going to work in jeans and T-shirts. They found it hard to reconcile this with the fact that I was still a police lady, and the vague answers I gave to their confused questions were not stemming their interest.

In the middle of tea one day, our six-year-old put down her fork, looked at me with a hard stare and asked, 'What *do* you do at work, Mummy?' She said it with an exasperated tone that added to the question, 'and don't fob me off with any of your usual flannel, this time tell me the truth.'

I looked her in the eye and said, 'Mummy looks after children who have been upset or hurt at home.'

Now she was confused, and sat silently for a few minutes trying to work this one out – I could see her child-like imagination trying to make sense of what appeared to her to be a contradictory sentence. She could accept that a child might need a doctor or even a firefighter if they were upset or hurt at home, but she could not understand that they could ever need the police. After racking her brains for a while she asked, 'You mean if a burglar comes in and snatches their toy?'

Her innocence was beautiful and washed a tide of sadness over me for the millions of children whose childhood, crushed by abuse, can never be returned to them; all the helpless children who are brutalized without mercy to gratify the perversions of adults. Both our girls accept that Mummy goes to work to help children who have been hurt at home and they seem happy with that explanation for now.

A few inquisitive souls have asked me if working among pornographic material affects my own attitude to sex. All I can say is that John invariably has a smile on his face and hasn't lodged any complaints, so I guess not, eh?

. . . and a copper

After defining myself as a Christian, a wife and a mother, I finally get round to saying that I am a copper.

My current role within the police challenges and satisfies many of my (and, I believe, every copper's) professional requirements. In lots of ways, I can't think of another role within the organization that I'd rather do. Many police officers ask me the 'How do you do your job?' question with as aghast a tone as anyone else, and I know they are referring to managing the images. But there's so much more to the job that is fantastic and, the images aside, I reply that they don't know what they're missing.

Police officers have the paradoxical privilege of stepping behind people's front doors and finding out what is really going on in their lives – it's a paradox because it can be as horrifying as it can be entertaining. The privilege breeds an innate nosiness which is always ready for the next front door, however incredible the last one was. In my Unit we go one better: we find out what goes on behind the bedroom door as well. Come on, don't tell me that wouldn't intrigue you just a tiny bit, too? We find it's like a morbid curiosity which is as frequently disgusted as it is amused; like reading the tabloids for free. With every case I come across I realize what an old prude I must be, for the sexual shenanigans of apparently staid and ordinary people could diminish the porn industry to the archives of boredom. It is relevant for us to delve into offenders' sexual behaviour, and the humour I have enjoyed in this Unit cannot be found anywhere else. I wouldn't have missed it for the world.

I don't know many folk – let alone coppers – who aren't fascinated to know just a little bit about what really goes in people's lives, and I certainly don't know many coppers who are not enthused by catching the bad guys. Surely that's why we go to work! And in our Unit we not only catch the bad guys, we bang on their doors in the early hours of the morning shouting, 'Police, police!' and haul them out of bed. None of them get away, none of them are expecting us, and all of them are mortified by our arrival. When you know this is a bloke who likes hurting children it is a great feeling to take away his liberty and pride in circumstances he finds so humiliating. And then, unlike so many other areas of policing that involve meticulous searches for evidence that are sometimes fruitless, our evidence is nicely sitting on the study desk waiting for us to pack it up at our leisure, store it away and analyse it as and when we are ready. That to me is job satisfaction running at a premium rate.

There is much humour in the office regarding the offenders we deal with and other aspects of the job. You have to have a stomach of steel to bear the level of humour sometimes plumbed, but the giggles are imperative to getting through the day and, as such, I am seldom offended. It is important to stress here that there is utter respect for the images and the children depicted in them. I have never heard an inappropriate word about them and never expect to. None of us pretend that the viewings are ever anything other than abhorrent, and we help each other out in coping with sessions that are difficult. I have never felt the need to hide distress and outwardly 'cope', and by their openness I presume that neither have my colleagues. That makes for a healthy working environment amid the unhealthy nature of our job, and enables us to ride the emotional storms caused by the images with the thunderous laughter evoked by so much else.

The police management acknowledges that viewing indecent images of children takes an emotional toll on those of us who undertake it. As well as the Child Protection Unit, we are the only officers who have compulsory counselling built into our job description. It is provided by the force Occupational Health Unit and we are required to attend a consultation with a counsellor every six months and then are encouraged to use the service at any other time we feel the need to. I have always found these sessions genuine and helpful. Outside of the office and my marriage there aren't many people who want to listen to the intricacies of my job, and having the chance to freely air how I feel is therapeutic in itself for me. The counselling protects the police management too because they have a duty of care towards our mental welfare, and we know that if we exhibit worrying signs of not coping in the Unit we could be moved. That is fair enough, but if we don't want to be moved we are careful about what we say. Two weeks before my first ever session I suffered a miscarriage but didn't say a word about it in my counselling – I didn't want to risk being moved.

One of the unspoken pressures of working in the Paedophile Unit is being cordial to offenders. We deal with some of the most distasteful people walking the planet, and when you know just how unpleasant they are – because they defile little children – the last thing you want to do is shake their hand, chat about the weather and make a cup of tea. The only way I am able to do so is to think of the children. If I told a pervert what I thought of him I'd lose the case – believe me, I'd lose the case. I would cross so many lines I would lose my job, actually, let alone the case! But that loss would still be peanuts compared to what the children would lose. Every conviction is a chance to help them just a tiny bit and I couldn't live with my conscience if I allowed my personal feelings to jeopardize the chance of some justice for them. I care passionately about trying to help the victims I see in the images, so I bite my lip, I smile a bit (can't manage sweetly) and I treat offenders with a courteous professionalism. I have to walk away from work with my self-respect intact and, most importantly, I have to honour the children.

Another dimension to remaining professional with sex offenders is being in a position to glean as much from them as possible during interview. When I have them in police custody it is the only time they are on my territory, on my terms, and I have a purpose to achieve – I want to know as much as I can get them to tell me. The more respectful I am towards them, the better my chances of sowing some seeds of rapport to be ploughed in the interview. During those minutes of taped discussion I am the boss, and things have to proceed as I want them to, at my pace. I plan interviews carefully and know exactly what I want to achieve and the different tactics I am going to employ. Upsetting the offender prior to interview is not a good tactic at all. I want to keep him as well disposed as I can, so I am polite to him until the interview starts and then I employ whatever tactic the law allows to tear down his defences. (Though I did rebuff one sex offender because he tried to chat me up while we were waiting to book him into custody at the nick. Ugh.)

There is a strange privilege to working in the Paedophile Unit which I was grateful to discover at the end of my first week. I think God was showing me the perks of my job as well as the challenges early on. On the Friday concerned I had worked with a colleague to interview a suspect who was answering bail after his computer equipment had been analysed. A significant quantity of indecent images had been discovered and when questioned he made full confessions regarding the material and openly discussed his lifelong sexual interest in little girls.

The following day, John and I took our daughters to a large military air show some distance from our home. It was a lovely event which was thoroughly enjoyed by us all (though I do not recommend going to the Ladies in a portable cabin at the precise moment a fighter jet booms overhead. I learnt that Portakabins reverberate uncontrollably in these conditions and it is difficult to remain seated). We were having our picnic lunch among lots of other people, sitting on the grass when, with a mouth full of sandwich, I looked up and saw the paedophile in question walking by with extensive camera equipment slung over his shoulders. Our eyes locked in a gaze for about two seconds, and he was the one to turn away. I continued to stare at him as he glanced down at the grass, threatening with my glare: *'If you take a second glance at my girls, you're mincemeat, pal.'*

He skulked off, well aware that I was pointing him out to John. We now felt like the luckiest parents of the thousands present at the show. We were privileged to know that he was a paedophile: a paedophile with a camera among lots of children; a paedophile who blended in among lots of other photographers. Who was to know if he was taking pictures of children or planes? Believe me, if I could have followed him round with a loudspeaker shouting, *'pervert alert, pervert alert'* I would have done , but the Data Protection Act put his privacy before the protection of children and so I was prevented from doing so. I don't know what he did or did not get up to that day, but I do know that I felt privileged to have been able to identify the danger that was in my daughters' midst. It's a strange perk to the job, but it's a valuable one.

So you see, like most other people I find policing the world of indecent images as revolting as it is fascinating, as isolating as it is compelling. There is much that I love about what I do – just as fervently as I loathe the images. The children are my driving force, and finding them some justice is deeply rewarding. Without my faith in God I could not undertake my duties at all, because I rely completely on his presence to function effectively amid the evil of child sexual abuse. My daily experience of him as a powerful living God is the most fascinating and compelling part of my work above anything else.

You couldn't make it up

One busy Friday evening, before I joined the Paedophile Unit, I was alone on uniformed police patrol in my panda car. The emergency calls were coming in thick and fast and, as usual, there were far more callers than coppers. I had just dealt with a confused ninety-three-year-old who had been fleeced of his pension, when I was sent to a nearby flat to deal with a burglary. On my arrival I was met by a smart young man sitting patiently in a car outside the flat who explained the following story as calmly as he could for someone who was highly exasperated.

The flat's tenant was an elderly asylum seeker from the Middle East, residing in Britain under the care of a refugee charity. The smart young man worked for this charity, and they had been letting their flat to the elderly asylum seeker under an official tenancy agreement. That had expired weeks earlier, but he was refusing to leave. Earlier that day he had gone out and, when charity staff arrived to clean the flat for the next tenant, they presumed that he had left completely, so entered the property, bagged up his belongings and began cleaning the mess. Then he returned, and he was not amused. He decided that the charity staff were burglars and, in a state of acute agitation, he called the police. It is fair to say that the elderly asylum seeker was an unstable man.

That's when I arrived – and in my professional opinion this was not a burglary. The charity staff had entered their own flat lawfully and stolen nothing – the only person transgressing was the occupant himself. I tried to diffuse the intensity of his raging temper, but his claims to have been on the telephone to the Queen, the Prime Minister, and various heads of State from the Middle East did not help the coherency of our debate. In the end I had to leave him stewing in his own juice and, after updating the smart young man from the charity still waiting patiently in his car, I left the address and flew across town to the next incident.

A few weeks later I received an official complaint notification at work – my first one in years of operational policing. I was instructed to attend force headquarters and advised to bring a solicitor with me. I was dumbfounded and could not fathom what I was being accused of; surely I would have remembered thumping someone or stealing any gold bullion in the course of my duties.

At force headquarters I met with my solicitor then went in for my tape-recorded interview. I was formally cautioned in the way of a prisoner under arrest, and then the Inspector investigating me read out the charges, all being levelled at me by the elderly asylum seeker:

1. I had received a bribe from the charity worker.
2. I had sexually harassed the asylum seeker.
3. I had failed to record and investigate a crime.

I burst out laughing, emphatically denying the first two, and dismissing the third on the basis that there was no crime committed to record and investigate! The police complaints department and the CPS then took months to finally decide that I did not receive any bribes – apparently I took £200 from the charity worker to refrain from arresting him for burglary – and I did not sexually harass the asylum seeker. This was the bit that intrigued me the most. I wondered what on earth he was going to say I had done; besides the fact that I am a happily married woman, he just wasn't my type. It was all rather disappointing in the end; apparently the totality of my harassment was that I looked at him and asked with a seductive tone, 'Are you lonesome tonight?'

My reply to that accusation was that it was an unsult – if I was going to harass the man I would have done a better job of it than that.

The complaint that I failed to record and investigate a crime remains upheld on my personal file – I have fiercely contested it on the basis that there was no offence, but Home Office rules dictate that I should have recorded the incident as a crime and then deleted it as a 'no crime'. This laborious process would have taken over two hours on the computer and another hour of paperwork during a frantic Friday night. That makes the bribery and harassment seem like the sensible option.

6.

The Monster of the Internet

I arrived at work one morning and was heading for the kettle when a colleague trampled on my plans by announcing that we were going out on an enquiry 'right now'. As a self-respecting employee I did not usually lift a finger without a caffeine injection, and my one-track mind struggled to process this interruption as I asked, 'I presume that "right now" means after I've put some coffee in my veins? I'm not too worried about blood as long as there's— '

'No, Rebecca, we're going out *right now*. I've just been sent a job from another force about a German man who's been grooming little girls on the Internet. The police got him just before he snatched one from a meeting he had engineered with her and in his computer they've found loads of other kids he's grooming. One of them lives near here and we need to speak to her and her parents as soon as possible.'

The coffee lost its crucial status on hearing that and, with descriptive choruses from other colleagues about how delicious their own drinks were (most unnecessary and something I wouldn't dream of doing to them), I ruefully left the office and we set off on the enquiry. During the journey to the girl's house I began considering the video interview I would be conducting with her, and we both bemoaned the dangers of chat rooms and websites yet again. A conversation along these lines is as standard to my working day as coffee.

We arrived at the smart terraced house and the front door was opened by an elderly lady who we presumed was the grandmother of the child. Then a few incisive questions changed everything. There was no child.

The young girl being groomed on the Internet by the German offender was a thirty-six-year-old man living at home with his mum. Mr J was a loner who spent hours upstairs on the computer, and Mum was thrilled that over recent months he had acquired a girlfriend – a single mother with young girls he was now 'fathering'. Mum was also thrilled that his one hobby involved volunteering for a local charity group, but this thrill was instantly lost (along with the 'fathering' one) when we clarified that his only role at the group was training youngsters: Mr J was not involved with any other area of the charity's work.

So it became clear that the German was pretending to be a child and grooming Mr J, to which Mr J was responding by pretending to be a child and grooming the German. If they weren't so dangerous I'd laugh at them for being such a pair of idiots.

You don't need to be a detective to realize that we stumbled upon a paedophile that morning and not an endangered child; well, except the endangered little girls Mr J was grooming through dating their mother, the teenage volunteers who formed his 'hobby' and the youngsters we later discovered he was talking to in children's chat rooms on the Internet. Examination of his computer showed that he used several chat room personas, all supported by accompanying photographs. He would cultivate a child through pretending to be a child himself, and then cement his grooming by sending them a photograph claiming to be the child depicted. The photos became progressively indecent – all downloaded from the Internet – and, in claiming to be the child in the picture, he could encourage children to respond with indecent acts of their own in front of their web-cams, as dictated by him. Mr J's personas and photographs covered a wide age range and included males and females: he was ready and waiting to prey on anyone.

The Internet is powerful. It has an inexhaustible ability to deceive and, as such, it is ideal for paedophiles: through a variety of Internet outlets they can indulge their *sexual attraction to children*, they can maintain the *strictest control*, and they can be *supremely devious*. The Internet is as perfectly designed for paedophiles as coffee is for mornings.

Note to single mothers: last week I laid a newspaper out on the floor to do some decorating and read the 'Lonely Hearts' column in the process. I was horrified to see how many women were advertising the fact that they were single with children and asking strangers into their lives. Some entries even had helpful descriptions of the children which were tantamount to gift-wrapping the poor things and tagging the package with a pretty label. Anyone with children who is dating needs to be extra-vigilant, not extra-honest.

'Lonely Hearts' columns, social Internet sites, dating agencies and the like enable abusers to shop around for children in the comfort of their own home, then move in for the kill on a person – usually a mother – who they know is keen to invite them in and make the relationship work. The recipe goes like this: Children can be perceived as a barrier to Mum finding new relationships, so appreciation of her offspring is a cast-iron way through the doors of her home and her heart. The children themselves might not like the new boyfriend, so grooming mechanisms can be passed off as genuine attempts to secure their hard-won acceptance and, if the kids complain when the abuse starts, they can be scorned for rejecting the new bloke and making up horror stories to scupper him. Most potently of all, the paedophile reminds Mum how much these horror stories scupper *her own* happiness and so the children become the troublemakers. She begins to resent them for sabotaging her golden opportunity with this lovely man who has tried so hard to please these ungrateful brats – his words, not hers. He gains the upper hand in Mum's thinking as the children become the problem, and he mutates the conspiracy he is executing against the kids into a conspiracy they are executing against him.

I'm sorry to put it so horribly, but it *is* so horrible. Anyone entering the dating scene with children would be wise to consult trusted friends about new partners – the head and the heart are just too unreliable. Paedophiles know this too, and plot their approach to the mother just as precisely as to the children; they will distort her judgement by exploiting the myriad of other factors buzzing around at the beginning of a friendship and especially a romance. If you are in this position, strengthen the protective guards you place around your children by at least ten-fold; *you cannot be too suspicious* – if anyone says you are, then suspect them.

Dark alleys

I do not allow my children to walk alone down dark alleys at night. In fact, I do not allow my children to walk alone down sun-drenched alleys during the day, just as I do not allow them to roam the streets and interact with any passing strangers they meet on the way, particularly ones concealing their identity. I do not allow my children to visit places I know nothing about, places where they can become embroiled in risky activities and then hide what they've been doing where I can't find out about it. Most of all, I am confident that I know far more about walking the streets, visiting strange places and frequenting dark alleys than they do. That's exactly why I don't allow my children free rein to explore the Internet. It is no different to any of these principles.

When children are on the Internet unsupervised it is exactly the same as them wandering down a dark alley all alone. In fact, I think it's worse. Most of the perverts we fear down dark alleys now prey on children through computers and aren't actually in the alley. Children have a level of alertness towards danger approaching them in dark places, but they are complacent about the mortal threat stalking them on their computers. Their defences are down, their vulnerability heightened. And, while most parents do not let their children wander dark alleys all alone, some leave them unsupervised for hours on the computer with no idea what they're doing, whereabouts they're doing it or who they're doing it with. In an Internet chat room, children are in the most critical of dark alleys – they are up for grabs to the thousands of highly skilled child abusers permanently prowling cyberspace solely to find a child. The computer is not a babysitter, it is not a toy, it is not just educational, and it is not a child's right: it is an extremely dangerous place. Because so many parents leave their children alone on the computer, so many paedophiles hunt for children on the computer. It's far more rewarding for them than lurking in dark alleys.

Prior to joining the Paedophile Unit, a colleague asked me to conduct some video interviews with three

ten-year-old girls who had been groomed on the
Internet and persuaded to perform sexual acts in front of
their webcam. At first I couldn't understand why they
had agreed to the indecent behaviour, and then I chided
myself for falling into the trap: *'They're immature children,
Rebecca; it's different for them.'*

'Maturity' is such a weak spot for pre-adolescents.
They desperately want to be 'mature': this has so much
mileage for exploitation, especially when their perception of 'maturity' is itself so *im*mature. Hey, my daughters think thongs and mascara represent maturity! Using
this weak spot paedophiles persuade little girls that they
really are the young ladies they aspire to be; Mum and
Dad are such spoilsports for not recognizing how grown
up they've become. In fact, of all the adults in the child's
circle, the paedophile is probably the only one pander-
ing to this deep longing: at surface level the child wants
to be what the paedophile is trying to make them.
Impressionable youngsters are easily enticed into behaving beyond their years when their understanding of
maturity is drawn from pop stars gyrating, film stars
pouting, TV stars groping, magazine stars stripping – far
from having to be persuaded to behave indecently, for
some children it is like living out the dream . . . at first.
But the illusion is soon shattered when the nightmare
dawns.

Performing in front of a camera for the pleasure of
drooling admirers is what children aspire to achieve in
some shape or form. It's a sign of arrival, recognition,
appeal, acceptance, and it feeds a hungry desire grum-
bling away inside most human beings. Come on, ladies,
don't tell me you've never paraded in front of a mirror
with two grapefruits stuffed down your top (I hoped for
greater things than satsumas), your skirt hitched up as
high as you dare, Mum's lipstick streaked around your

mouth and a hairbrush in your hand. Oh, you haven't?
Oh. Must have just been me, then. How embarrassing.
I'll make sure the editor deletes that sentence. [Hmmm
. . . I think we'll leave this in, Rebecca! Ed]

The video interviews I conducted with the three girls
were a sobering learning curve for anyone who cares for
children. The group comprised the girl at whose home
the offences took place, her best friend and her cousin.
Their parents were very supportive – within being mortified – but clearly a blame-game had broken out among
them as to which girl was the ringleader of events. I
reminded each set of parents that the paedophile was
the unequivocal ringleader, and apportioning blame to
the children played as much into his hands as the acts of
abuse. It excused him. The children were victims of their
natural vulnerability and if anyone was to blame after
the paedophile, it was the parents for being so slack.

The story began innocuously enough with the girls
having lots of tea and playtimes at each others' houses.
The first girl's house held the most appeal because she
had a computer in her bedroom, out of sight from her
parents. What bliss: being offered access to the whole
world without Mum and Dad sticking their nosey beaks
in! More and more the girls began to meet at the first
child's house and closet themselves away in her bedroom for hours on the computer. Each set of parents had
spotted this changing pattern of behaviour and not one
had challenged it; those whose kids were out visiting
enjoyed the break, and those being visited enjoyed the
peace the computer provided. I would have thought it
was fairly obvious that the children weren't doing their
maths homework up there; the length of time they were
left to their own devices was disturbing enough – hours
and hours, day after day – so either they were about to
graduate in economics, or something untoward was

going on. (I doubt any of those parents would have left
the girls unattended in a dark alley for very long.)

Of course something untoward was going on. They
had joined a children's chat room and were having a ter-
rific time interacting with a group of lads a few years
older than them, apparently. Paedophiles aren't daft.
They have to pitch their approach just right. If they present as being too advanced they could scare the children
off: ten-year-old girls are likely to be warier of older folk
who are beyond their social radar, and disinterested in
their own peers who offer limited flattery. To ensnare
children, paedophiles must appeal to them, so this one
presented as a group of thirteen-year-olds to capture his
prey. He pitched it perfectly – of course.

When the paedophile was satisfied with his groundwork, the innocent chat became risqué, then it became
naughty, and then it plumbed the downright explicit.
After that, the chat became actions and, within a few
weeks, all three girls were exposing themselves to the
webcam and doing various things to each other as
requested by the 'thirteen-year-olds'. Now they were
entrenched because they had gravely misbehaved, and
they knew their parents would hit the roof if their antics
were discovered. Along with delivering this threat,
which was cleverly veiled as a kind warning, the 'thirteen-year-olds' had sent photos of themselves – 'it was
definitely them', I was assured by each girl in interview.
'The boys' spoke the school lingo and didn't talk like
adults at all; no big words or tellings-off. They knew all
about the pop charts and teenage TV programmes – not
the stuff adults know about these days; oh yes, it was
definitely them.

It didn't enter their heads that an adult could masquerade as a child so convincingly. It was only when the
girls were asked to meet 'the boys' that one of them

became uneasy and made some remarks to her mum which prompted the whole investigation. What began as innocent chat in a children's chat room could have become the abduction and worse of three young girls.

On the computer, paedophiles are better at being children than children. Kids often try to appear older then they are and wind up out of their league, eventually falling foul of their own pretence. Paedophiles don't step out of the age-group they are copying; it is an art form they must master to fulfil their fantasies and they do so with Oscar-winning prowess. Paradoxically, the more of a child the child appears, the more of an adult they may actually be. Offenders spend huge amounts of time reading children's chat in chat rooms and learning the latest trends from language to music, from diet to fashion, from text-speak to sex-speak. When they start conversing with a child they keep it squeaky clean, so if they are revealed as an impostor they can easily retreat. I've read exchanges where it has been the child who has introduced a saucy comment, and the masquerading paedophile has feigned childish shock and confusion at the rudeness. This concretes his disguise while he gladly logs the development as a great vehicle through which to intensify the grooming when he's ready. Perverts repeatedly test their progress, and only when they are confident that their child-speak is sufficiently honed will they move the grooming up a gear.

Just for a minute imagine being in the car with a woman driver: she slides through the gears with such beautiful and seamless transition you don't notice it happening. Now put a bloke in the driver's seat and, crunch! You lurch forward with every gear change, cricking your neck backwards in an effort not to activate the airbag . . . OK, fair enough, so while the woman was beautifully changing gear she didn't notice the juggernaut that was lumbering towards her, point taken. When the pae-dophile 'goes up a gear' it's a woman's kind of gear change – subtle but deadly.

When he first engages with a child he will often allow them to dictate the pace; he needs to glean as much information as he can and not appear too pushy. The grooming changes when the offender has the child's full trust and, all of a sudden, he starts to take obvious control. The child goes along with this shift of power – they don't even notice it – and are participating in explicit discussions, sexual actions, exchanges of phone numbers and even meetings without logging the danger. The child knows they shouldn't do these things with strangers – but this isn't a stranger, it's a lovely new friend who has empowered them to sit in the driving seat of the friendship. At some point the offender may give away his true identity – he has to if he wants to deepen the involvement – but that isn't done until the child is so steeped in wrongdoing and allegiance that they are compelled to keep the secret. The paedophile may have waited and trained for years for this moment. Don't forget that they put their whole lives on the line when they strike, so they don't strike lightly.

Some older children knowingly interact with a per-vert on the computer like playing 'chicken' with a bus. Fully aware of the danger, they are excited by the naugh-tiness, and place undue confidence in their own ability to maintain control. Dashing in front of buses always brings the risk of being flattened: 'But I'll be fine, I'm not so silly as to actually get run over. It's just a bit of a laugh.' Similarly from Internet chat-logs I have read, some teenagers know they are in the danger zone but clearly think they can extricate themselves from this pathetic pervert if necessary. They even con themselves into believing that it is them playing games at the expense of the offender: 'He's just a wimpy pervert. I'm a streetwise lass; he's no match for me.' But as with the bus, the youngster inevitably gets flattened because they lose control. Not many child abusers are as stupid as their target thinks them to be, and the ones who appear so are probably particularly clever ones who have used 'stupidity' as the main ingredient of their recipe. It's not a bad ploy when you think about it. (I've used it myself, actually. I once interviewed a child abuser who clearly saw me and thought 'female = useless'. I managed to contain my indignation at his obvious chauvinism and theatrically fed his prejudice by appearing to forget things and drop things so he could continue to write me off as incompetent. Once we were in the taped interview I let my façade of uselessness run a bit longer – please don't ask 'What façade?' – and then I turned turtle and gave him the pistol-whipping of an interview he deserved. For a man who repeatedly thrashed his young son with a poker he got off lightly.)

Much as we throw our hands up in horror when a child sex offender strikes through the Internet, I think it is a miracle they don't strike more often, considering the amount of freedom children are given online. Lack of parental control has a lot to do with children being groomed on the Internet and, if children were not allowed to roam the web uncontrolled, they would not be so vulnerable to attack.

My most recent investigation concerned a retired man in his early sixties. Mr K was an overweight individual who walked slowly in evident discomfort. He told me that in addition to his pension he received disability benefit for a back injury sustained during his working years, but I'm not convinced that work was to blame. He spent such a crippling amount of time cemented into his computer chair I reckon that when he stood up the chair came with him, which was probably what was causing the pain.

Mr K's case originated via a website designed for school pupils to engage with each other online. Safeguards were in place regarding impostors, but if someone is determined to infiltrate a website for children they will find a way – and Mr K did. If hackers can break into the fortified websites of government they can certainly break into youngsters' play zones. A host of information systems provide sufficient data about schools. I could probably pose as a pupil of most establishments nationwide and wheedle my way into a website of this ilk, and I'm as great with computers as Mr K is with a rowing machine.

Mr K easily set himself up as a school pupil and was soon chatting up young teenage girls like there was no tomorrow. And when I say 'chatting up' I'm talking the cheesiest drivel you've ever read. What he wrote was wretched; the cheese was dripping so copiously from every line I nearly ordered a round of toast and some Worcester sauce.

A number of girls were either distressed or entertained by Mr K's approaches, and their complaints finally found their way to the police. The route their complaints took was longwinded, and it was a parent who contacted us in the end. Relying on children and teenagers to raise the alarm is not a protective system any adult should depend upon. As we saw from the three girls earlier, children are reluctant to instigate complaints for many obvious reasons, but the not-so-obvious one is the most compelling of all: by the time a youngster is alarmed by someone on the Internet they have usually engaged in some form of misbehaviour with them – *crucially, not many perverts will cross the decency line without taking the child with them.* By raising the alarm, children incriminate themselves – so, to avoid the fallout, most just don't raise the alarm. Mr K had contacted a large number of girls and, due to the sheer volume of his operation, it gradually seeped out from the teenager's circle and into adult ears. To this day I don't know if the girls are aware that one of their parents informed the police, that we have read all their chat-logs and taken formal action against Mr K.

During his police interview, Mr K told me that he spent seventeen hours a day on his computer in children's chat rooms. Seventeen hours a day! He had no life but the thrill of grooming children on the Internet; it was the reason he breathed. However, I was even more shocked by the explanation he gave for such devotion: throughout the seventeen hours he could travel through various time zones and connect with children on a worldwide scale. This delighted him. He came to life as he excitedly talked, and it repulsed me to realize that simply putting it into words was catapulting his hormones into a flight path of their own. With eyes aglow he relished the fact that when the English kids went to bed the Australian ones woke up and he switched his attention to them. As the hands on his clock went round their dial, so the hands on his computer went round the world – that's the command of the Internet. Mr K is sitting out his lifetime in children's chat rooms hunting for your children. Don't leave them alone on the web because eventually he'll find them. And if he doesn't, one of the thousands like him will.

So what are we all to do? The monster of the Internet isn't going to go away, its appeal to children isn't going to go away, and neither is its appeal to dangerous predators. But the monster has an innate weakness because it has two ends that have to function together before it can bite – one end is the pervert's computer and the other end is the child's. The pervert's end can't be successful without the child's end groomed into submission. Sure, the pervert's end is beyond our control – but the child's end is not. That gives us the power back. If the child's end is effectively supervised, the monster is dealt a hammer blow.

It's all about the fire regulations principle. There are a host of best practices all childcarers can implement – however inconvenient at times – which massively reduce the risks our children face in the dark, dark alley of the Internet. If you want to protect your child online, you can. Stringent supervision equals stringent protection. Below are some of the measures John and I are taking to protect our daughters online; it's not perfect because no system is, but it is our best shot. It's also not always popular with our offspring but that's irrelevant; their safety comes before their entertainment.

- We need to know more about computers than the kids, which is easier said than done. My two were helping me use the mouse at the same time as I was helping them use the potty. I was a bit amused and a bit impressed – then ever so alarmed. The more they are ahead of me in their computer skills the more a paedophile can catch them streaking away from my protective mantle. Therefore I have been on a computer course to ensure I know as much as they do and don't add another link to the chain of vulnerability. If I am ignorant about computers, my children could exploit the freedom this offers them. And, because my children are ignorant about child protection, an abuser could exploit the freedom *this* offers *them*. I am confident that I can trace everything my children do on the computer, and if I ever think I am falling behind them I will educate myself to regain the ground.

- The children are not allowed secret passwords or usernames for any area of the computer they use. Access to the Internet can only be gained through my personal username which is heavily password protected – it's not that I don't trust the children, it's that I don't trust the perverts. Though, saying that, our eldest did try to buck the system once by hacking her way into an Internet connection – she was seven at the time. She made a complete hash of attempting what was impossible anyway, and I felt a bit hypocritical reprimanding her when inside I was chuffed to realize that the system works. As they get older our daughters may resent our control of Internet access, but we can live with that. What we can't live with is the notion of handing them a golden opportunity to waltz down a dark alley to be violated.

- Thus the children cannot use the Internet without my knowledge. They do have their own areas of the computer they can use offline, and these have passwords that John and I know. I sometimes check they haven't changed them and they know that the penalty for doing so would be severe. When the girls are online they have a list of approved websites from which they mustn't deviate and every website they go on is one I have familiarized myself with first. As they grow up and want to explore further I will check out what they are interested in before they join anything – I wouldn't send them down a dark alley without checking it was safe and the Internet is no different.

- The computer is located in a communal area of the house and always will be. No one needs to hide away on it, and the girls will be well advanced into their teen years (like nineteen and eleven months) before they are allowed a personal computer in their bedrooms.

- We keep updated with the best security software we can – it's so good it sometimes annoys us. Recently we wanted to find an article about kids' car seats that had been published in a parenting magazine. We tried to download it but the security mechanisms wouldn't play ball because the magazine also had an article with the word 'sex' in it and this was banned. Hey ho, I can find the article elsewhere, but again the system works and is worth every penny and occasional moment of personal inconvenience. Protecting children is not an inconvenience in the grand scheme of things.

- When the kids are on the computer I make sure I am around. I don't breathe down their necks – though they may beg to differ – but I am around. I want them to know that there's no point trying something daft, I want others to quickly discover that my kids are not up for grabs, and John and I are resolute that the computer must never become a childminder. Even when I am engaged on the computer with them the unexpected can happen. For example: our girls love going on 'Google Images' with us where they put in different words and enjoy trawling the pictures that come up. On one occasion we put in 'Easter eggs' and got something we didn't expect. Thankfully the pornographic image was so bizarre I had pressed delete before they had finished asking their puzzled: 'What's that, Mum?' Inputting 'Barbie' was worse. Nowhere is safe!

- Bringing up kids is a lifelong exercise in education. We give them constant education about the Highway Code, eating up their greens and washing their hands, and we also give our daughters constant education about the computer. I don't just mean operating it; I mean education about safety when they're using it.

We can't take anything for granted when they're at such risk. We make no secret of the fact that the Internet is not safe because unpleasant people use it for unpleasant reasons. I don't intend ever stopping this education. No, not even when *they* have to *walk me* across the busy street, liquidize *my* greens because my teeth have fallen out and help *me* to the sink from my commode.

Educating children about child protection matters is imperative to their safety, both online and in 'real life'. If we avoid the fact that there are monsters out there – lots of them and usually wearing innocent guises – we assist perverts to operate. It takes children a long time to get their heads round the fact that most 'naughty people' do not skulk around after dark wearing a stripy jumper and carrying a swag bag. Only two days ago, I was queuing to pay for petrol behind a man who stunk like a brewery. I watched him walk from the kiosk to his car and, once we were all back in our vehicles, John followed him for a distance while I was on my mobile phone reporting him to the police. The girls thought this was marvellous fun, but voiced their surprise that the driver was committing a criminal offence. He had been stylishly dressed and smiled at them on his way across the forecourt, his car was 'well smart, Mummy', his wife looked really pretty (not when he smashes her into a tree, she won't) and 'He doesn't look like a naughty man, Mum.' Not many naughty men do.

Stranger-danger education is only the introduction to teaching children about their own safety. As we have already seen, most sex offenders do not offend as a stranger, which limits the value of stranger-danger advice. Of course that foundation is vital, but once it has been firmly laid it needs a wall of information to be built upon it about the prevalent and far more subtle reality of how most child sex offenders execute their horror. In terms of the Internet that means childcarers need to know more about its potential than their children so that they are in a position to teach, to monitor and to troubleshoot.

Through my job I have learned a fair amount about computers, though the fancy stuff is still the domain of the High-Tech boys and they are supremely patient in delivering 'Idiot's Guides' to me on the frequent occasions I need them. I dread to think how much they roll their eyes as they walk away from yet another 'Computing-for-Noddy' kind of chat they have had to lower themselves to on my behalf. The aspects of the Internet I have learned about have been critical in understanding how to protect my own children – chat rooms, MSN messenger, peer-to-peer file-sharing folders, pop-ups, web cams, interactive websites. It shocked me to realize that I knew more about the chicken pox than these inventions, yet I dread the consequences of the computer far more. I'm not going to go into a technical explanation about the wealth of Internet facilities because I am not qualified to do so but you can bet your bottom dollar your child knows about them. And you can bet your bottom dollar your nearest paedophile knows – and statistically he is not far away. If you don't have a good working knowledge of what your computer offers, I urge you to go and educate yourself.

The education that is hardest to come by is the education we need the most: cracking the chat room codes devised against parental control. There is a dialect of abbreviations that children and teenagers use online – quickly mastered by offenders – that secretly warn others if an adult is about. Can you imagine how golden they are to paedophiles? A simple example is 'P.O.S.' If you walk in the room and your child types these letters they are telling everyone that there is a 'Parent Over Shoulder'. In a flash any illicit communication will stop, and you'll see quadratic equations being discussed instead of what went on behind the bike sheds at lunchtime. When you've gone, further codes alert everyone that the coast is clear, and the detail about the bike sheds can continue. If you read what you don't understand when your child is online, question it. Paedophiles need the codes, children enjoy the codes, so parents must conquer them. And let's not forget who foots the bill for all this! You pay for the computer and its costs; who's calling the shots? If our daughters want to indulge in secret codes they will find that two can play at that game – our secret codes will be the 'off' button losing its 'on' facility, and the computer going into retirement. Remember: what is done on a computer is done in the name of the person to whom it is registered. Any questionable activity will be attributed to them in the first instance. On more than one occasion I have mistakenly hauled a dad out of bed for what have later transpired to be the sins of his child.

The value of supervision and education is not just about protecting children from attack – there's another side to the unthinkable coin of child sexual abuse, and that's protecting children from becoming attackers. Over the years it seems to me that the Internet has offered youngsters a unique opportunity to become offenders themselves – youngsters who would not have been sucked into that spiral of crime without the murky currents of cyberspace to carry them. The current that draws them in is the standard mix of deception, secrecy, and poor supervision all fizzed up with lashings of hormones. The following case of Mr L exemplifies the danger all too well, though from here on we're going to call him Master L so that we never forget this lad was merely fifteen when he was arrested.

The information for the warrant originated from a young boy elsewhere in the country. Chat-logs from this boy's computer showed how aggressively Master L was grooming him and, as I read the logs, I built up a picture of Master L. He was clearly a domineering lad with a vivid sexual imagination, who had already cajoled the child into committing a number of indecent acts. The depth of his imagination was second only to the thorough control he had established over the child he was grooming. I was ready for an obnoxious young man. But I was in for a surprise.

In real life, Master L was the antithesis of his Internet persona. His parents were distraught that their quiet, law-abiding son was being arrested for anything, let alone paedophile offences: 'He never gives us any trouble. He's very studious and doesn't go out much. He wants to be a teacher and he's such a kind, thoughtful sort of lad. I couldn't wish for a gentler son.' So how did this teenage lamb end up in custody for being a beast?

It starts with a lack of supervision on behalf of his parents – who, I must add, were very lovely people. After the initial distress they set about helping their son with dignified honesty, and I have full admiration for them. They had allowed Master L to have a computer in his bedroom and were unaware that he was on it for hours at night after they had gone to bed. Their own computer proficiency was far beneath his and they didn't know what he was up to or how to find out. His lack of friendship was unaddressed and his increasing withdrawal from life around him was put down to the tribulations of his age.

He himself was quite socially inept and didn't make friends easily. Physically he had reached the gangly stage of puberty, and hormonally he was in a state of mayhem – but where that obstructed him in real life it didn't matter to the computer. In its removed world Master L could pretend to be everything he wasn't, and he lived his fantasies out so fully they became his reality. The computer took an addictive hold over him that offered escape from real life; it was all so false, so damaging, but it was so much easier than facing the rigours of school. In a chat room you can tell people you are a Brad Pitt look-alike with as much brain as brawn, and who knows that you've really got a stubborn acne problem, very little self-confidence and are falling behind in class? The deceptive qualities of the Internet can seriously impede the development and social skills of our children.

After his arrest, Master L's parents implemented all the measures they should have put in place years before – all of which I believe would have prevented him from straying into his offences. The new computer they bought was located in the kitchen where a freshly educated Mum and Dad controlled both the passwords and the length of time their children were allowed on it. Accountability was restored, and the family slowly recovered.

Contrast Master L with Master M. Master M was nasty to the core. A young teenager with a voracious appetite for indecent images of children, he had images of babies being brutalized. Through his computer he had begun dabbling in adult pornography at a young age – a huge number of lads do this and it seems to be widely accepted as a rite of passage. However, when you combine the confusions of puberty with the readiness of extreme online pornography this acceptance becomes far more concerning. Twenty years ago we may have been talking some top-shelf magazines; now we're talking unlimited material of the most depraved nature. If we let teenagers shape their understanding of sex through computers we are going to breed a multitude of disturbed sex offenders.

Master M quickly slipped down the irreversible slope from adult pornography into images of children – I call it 'irreversible' because I haven't come across many who have managed to climb back up. What started as a 'laugh' for the shock factor became an addiction that satiated his desire for extremity and domination. Master M became uncontrolled and uncontrollable. The computer was the only channel for his personality that did not thwart him – everywhere else he was in constant combat with authority figures, but not online. Through the Internet he could unleash his instincts and although I don't think the Internet caused Master M's offending in the way it did Master L, it certainly fuelled a fire that could have been otherwise contained. He was young enough that he could have been helped without the constant fanning into flame of his deviancy that the Internet provided.

The Internet is a dark alley where more danger lurks than we'll ever know. For most children, this is in the form of countless predators on a worldwide scale: for a few, it represents a chance to become one of them. There is little that Internet providers can do when offenders mostly parade as lawful children in lawful websites, there is little that police can do when we're so acutely under-resourced, and there is little that schools can do beyond a bit more education. I believe it's down to parents and carers. If we are supremely vigilant when our children are online, if we are adamant that the computer is a resource and not a right, and if we are determined not to succumb to its babysitter capacity we can reverse this monstrous tide. We have a choice: either we don't allow our children into the dark alley at all, or we accompany them when they're there. I fervently believe that children should only be allowed to use the Internet under the strictest of conditions that place supervision, education, and accountability long before the fun factors.

That way we can floodlight the alley.

You couldn't make it up

Last year a chap went through our Unit who was not very good at evading the police. This year he went through our Unit again because he still isn't very good at evading the police. In fact, I think we may have stumbled on the world's most hapless paedophile. There's no doubt that he is a paedophile – his sexual attraction to children is fearsome – it's just that he's not too clever at the 'control' and 'devious' bits. He just doesn't seem to be able to crack this police evasion thing.

When he first came to our notice he had already been caught possessing indecent images of children by his local police. His images were among some of the most appalling we have ever seen. He was finding his repeated capture a nuisance; his equipment kept being seized and he couldn't afford to shell out for constant replacements. After a while, he thought up the grand idea of using Internet cafés to indulge his perversion and, even grander than that – wait for it – he decided to buy a train ticket and travel a long distance away from home where his local police couldn't find him. Unfortunately for him he omitted to register that the whole country is policed by the same laws as his home town and that the cost of the train ticket wasn't far off the cost of a second-hand computer anyway. He arrived in our area and soon found an Internet café where he sat down to watch an afternoon of filth. He also omitted to register that the computer he chose was situated in the café window and he was viewing his filth in full sight of the shopping public – one of whom was an off-duty copper from our Unit who shopped him.

A few months later he tried to learn from his mistakes – no mean feat considering their number – and he acquired a USB stick. This is a very small device that can hold large amounts of computer information, and he filled his stick with thousands of indecent images of children. This plan went pear-shaped when he kept the stick in his wallet for safe-keeping, then lost his wallet. It contained his name and address alongside the offending USB stick and he was quickly traced.

7.

Female Abusers: The Ultimate Taboo?

'Women are the fairer sex' – or so the saying goes. If I'm honest I've never quite understood the meaning of that; fairer in what way? Loads of women have dark hair so they're not fairer than all the blond blokes, and the darker-skinned women in the world are not fairer than the lighter-skinned men. The hormonal roundabout doesn't make females fair-tempered on occasions and, from estate agents to magistrates, I wouldn't say that women are any fairer than men when making their judgements. The weather isn't fairer when women are around, so how exactly are women fairer? Oh surely not the old childbirth thing? There is absolutely nothing fair about that! It's an undignified process; never have I felt more like I belonged in jungle scrub than when I was giving birth. And what was fair about John watching me in agony while he reclined in a chair eating the box of chocolates intended to sustain me through labour? True, he did leave me the orange crème but only because he doesn't like them, though to be fair – excuse the pun – I did have the chance to even the score recently when I picked him up from his vasectomy appointment and drove home over the speed bumps. Which brings us to another saying: the one about women and the fury they can muster when they deem themselves scorned. There's rarely much fairness about that.

Through my job I have been shaken to learn that where child sexual abuse is concerned, women are no more exclusively the fairer sex than in any other area of life.

I believe that God created the world just as the Bible says he did, which means he purposefully created women to be both different and complementary to men. I know that God delights in all the things – contrary or otherwise – that make women uniquely women, and he loves each one of us with unfathomable depth. One of my favourite demonstrations of this is that on the glorious morning when Jesus rose from the dead, he chose to appear to a woman first (Mk. 16:9). It was one of the most remarkable encounters in the whole of history and he chose to share it with a woman. And not just any woman. No, he chose someone who had been a real sinner-type of girl. I love that. It tells us so much about him.

I think the Bible endorses God's passion for women constantly, and one prominent channel of this is through our God-given capacity to love and nurture children. There are countless references to this special gift throughout the pages and ages of the Bible; take Isaiah 66:13 for example. For those of you unfamiliar with the Bible, Isaiah was a prophet whose contribution to the Book was written hundreds of years before the birth of Christ. The aforementioned verse is one where God is speaking through Isaiah about how much he loves his people and longs to take care of them. After a number of descriptive analogies God says that the way a mother comforts her child is the way that he will comfort his people. He doesn't need to expand on the explanation; he knows that such strong imagery will paint the picture he is drawing in the richest of colours.

Stop and think about it. God: the One who made the universe, whose magnitude is beyond words, whose eternal love is beyond understanding, whose immeasurable power is without limit – he likens his commitment to humankind to a woman comforting a child. That makes women and children powerful stuff.

I think something goes particularly wrong when a woman sexually abuses a child. The perversion is perverted just a little bit more than when a man commits the offence. Perhaps that means I've got some prejudice issues to iron out; perhaps it's just because I'm a woman myself. But I can only tell you that when I have seen images of women sexually abusing children and dealt with female offenders it turns something in my stomach just a little bit tighter than the male offenders manage to twist it.

The case of Ms N

My first ever case in the Child Protection Unit involved a female offender. I wasn't ready for her. I had few professional defences in place when it came to engaging with Ms N and was functioning on that easy presumption that a few terrible men sexually abuse children and women just don't. It's a foolish presumption that facilitates female abuse as much as anything else; how many of us are wary of strange men but switch our antennae to stand-by mode for a woman? The presumption is helpful for male offenders too; parade a woman to switch off the antennae then offend while no one's concentrating. Ian Brady and Myra Hindley/Fred and Rose

West are extreme examples of this principle at work, but they are by no means unique.

Ms N was living with her latest man in a small well-kept apartment. She had custody of her four-year-old daughter I'll call Janie, and had peppered the child's life with a succession of boyfriends following the breakdown of her marriage to Janie's father. The poor child had become a pawn in their acrimonious divorce, and was moved back and forth as they used her to score points against each other in their feud. Janie herself was one of the few children I have met who could have persuaded me to become a primary school teacher. The little girl was so bright, so bubbly and so beautifully innocent that I wondered if she was actually real or had just stepped out of a nursery-rhyme book.

Being my first ever case, she became my first ever video interview and I was terrified. I knew that officers interviewing a child get one bite at the evidential cherry and if they make a mistake, they've lost. But that's not where the terror comes from – the terror comes from the fact that it's the child's loss. The consequences of making a mistake are as awesome as the potential held in a successful interview, and the barriers between the interviewer and a truthful account are many – fear, misunderstanding, embarrassment, shame, terror, power, obligation, threats – all falling under the most hazardous denominator of all which is a child's perspective and expression. As we saw earlier, childishness and courtroom etiquette are not compatible, and the bridge traversing the huge gulf between them has to be crossed by the interviewer . . . at the first attempt.

I needn't have worried. Janie sat and cuddled her doll while she told me how Ms N and her boyfriend had beaten her up and sexually misused her. The man had instigated the incident and manipulated the mother to 'take sides' – and she had chosen her violent boyfriend over her vulnerable daughter. I hardly had to ask Janie any questions, she bravely dominated the interview and I listened in horrified silence as she articulated her nightmare with precision. Janie had suffered a sustained attack during which she had been badly beaten, rammed against furniture, held under cold water, stripped, verbally defiled, and held aloft by her throat. Her pleas for mercy were mocked by both adults as she was forced to crouch under the table like an animal, thumped when she wet herself through fear and their refusal to grant toilet access, and placed naked and shivering outside. A sexual dimension was added to the assault through mocking Janie's naked body and forcing her to do things to herself.

The following day, all of Janie's bruises came out, leaving precious little of her body its original colour. Seeing her daughter so brutalized did not wash waves of remorse over Ms N, it provoked a dilemma about how to conceal the damaged condition Janie was in. I still don't understand how she saw her child's battered skin and only wanted to save her own. Ms N's contempt for her daughter deepened when she was faced with the choice of taking Janie to playgroup and risking discovery, or being lumbered with the girl at home all morning. The 'being lumbered all morning' bit appeared more troublesome to her than her own guilt, so she caked Janie's injuries in thick make-up to disguise them and packed her off to playgroup for some peace. Of course the child looked ridiculous – she would have been overdressed for a pantomime. So much make-up was needed to conceal so many bruises that the staff would have been guilty of neglect themselves if they had not spotted the strange appearance of this beautiful child. They raised the alarm and Janie was taken into care.

It was my job to arrest and interview both Ms N and her boyfriend. The case was a long time ago now, but I recall being as shocked at Ms N's lack of regret as I was at the individual offences. She had consciously aligned herself with the boyfriend's brutality; no amount of reasoning with her seemed able to ignite the faintest spark of feminine care towards Janie. To be honest, I think she was glad to be shot of the poor girl. Both abusers were found guilty at court and a subsequent baby born to them was taken from their care at birth.

Women who sexually abuse children are very rare and among their number those who abuse alone are particularly unusual, constituting a minute proportion. In my experience, women are usually operating in conjunction with someone – while men often operate as a lone ranger – and I have always found that someone to be a man. It follows that I have always found that man to be a paedophile.

I learned something through Ms N that has been concreted into my thinking with every female child abuser I have since encountered. It's by no means an exclusive theory but it has been the foundation of every case I have personally dealt with. In my opinion, female sexual abuse begins when the woman makes a fatal choice between a man and a child. More often than not she finds herself in a position between the two – maybe domestically, professionally, socially, or even strategically as in 'stranger' cases. The origin of her offences lies in allegiance to the man, and a chasm opens up before her with him on one side and the child on the other. She chooses which one of them to align herself with and it's a straightforward choice: either she puts herself first or she puts the child first. When she chooses the man's side it is not primarily *him* she is choosing – it is *her own* well-being. The choice can appear complex because it is usually mired in difficult factors, but it's actually incredibly simple: 'Me or the kid.'

If she puts herself first, she chooses the man and the child is doomed. If she puts the child first, she walks away often at great cost to herself but the child is safe and the feminine bond set in steel, as it should be. There is rarely any room for compromise, and that's the position Ms N found herself in. She had a choice: she could either flout the boyfriend and protect Janie – risking harm to herself – or she could align herself with the boyfriend and abandon the child. The decision she came to was an indefensible one, beyond most people's understanding, but maybe without the boyfriend and his enforced chasm, Ms N wouldn't have served time in the clink for such serious child abuse. Granted, she wouldn't have won any mother-of-the-year awards either; she was always going to betray Janie because of her capacity to be so selfish and vicious. But it took his demand for a choice to propel her into activating it on the wrong side of the chasm. I wonder if she would have sunk so *horribly* low if she had stayed with Janie's father; when they were together there was no record of Ms N maltreating Janie and I'm sure he would have used any reports against Ms N in their marital feud if they had been there to use. The notorious stranger cases we know from the media all contain this fatal decision. Although not in an ongoing relationship with the child, the women chose to remain loyal to their men and themselves rather than adhere to God's principle of a woman caring for a child.

Three summaries

The characteristics of a paedophile that we have discussed so far – sexual attraction to children, control and deviousness – all feature for female abusers to various degrees but I think they stem from the original choice rather than lie at the cause of it. The principle can be the same for women who violate children in other ways but, for the purposes of this book, we are going to look at the women I have dealt with who have become embroiled in sexual abuse of children.

My theory presupposes that the woman is in a set-up where there is a man and a child to choose between. Well, every woman I have dealt with for sexually abusing a child has been in that set-up in some form, from mothering the child through to having no known relationship with them, as in those who view indecent images on the Internet – those women still have a choice between aligning with the man and watching the material, or aligning with the children and rejecting it. My colleague did once deal with an exception to prove my rule and I will close the chapter with a look at her, but here are three summaries of female sexual abusers. When you read them watch out for the point where she makes her choice, and afterwards we'll take a look at the unbearable 'why' question: a question I'm sure the children asked when they were older, and a question I hope the women asked long before. How they answered it I do not know.

1. Mrs O

I have to put Mrs O into context if I am to tell her story properly. I am being very polite when I say that Mrs O and her husband were both tickets short of a traffic warden, though in possession of useful amounts of cunning and control when it came to executing their offences. They had notable criminal histories and were so anti-police they had changed their surname by deed-poll to a ludicrous double-barrelled name containing over twenty letters of the alphabet. The sole reason they did this was to irritate the police every time they were arrested, because they knew that officers have to write out a detainee's name repeatedly. This was their idea of revenge.

'That's fine,' I remember saying to Mrs O when she explained it to me with an annoyingly smug look on her face, 'and here's mine.' I held up the big brass cell-door key and added: 'The longer I spend writing your name out, the longer you spend in there.' My turn to wear the annoyingly smug look!

Mrs O knew that Mr O was a paedophile and she was keen for him not to abuse their own children, so she reasoned that her best bet was to instigate situations in which he could abuse other people's. The couple decided to advertise themselves as registered childminders, guessing they would easily ensnare a child because parents would naturally trust Mrs O. They claimed to have all the relevant training and vetting, but no one ever checked this out because one of the pair was a woman. The mother of the girl they abused acknowledged to me that if Mr O had been working alone or if he had been half of a male partnership, she and her partner would have thoroughly investigated his claims, but they were hoodwinked by what they took as Mrs O's endorsement of him, solely because she was female.

Within days of a scribbled advert in a shop window, Mr and Mrs O were in charge of a five-year-old girl who lived across the road and, within days of taking charge, were indecently assaulting her. The assaults began as Mr O alone, but Mrs O was encouraged by him to join in the abuse and she complied. Her compliance became pleasure and she began to enjoy the offences as much as he did – indeed it was her idea to expand their business interests and advertise for another child. They were going to use their 'success' with the current one as their basis for attracting another. If this set of parents were happy, the next set could be assured that their child was in safe hands.

The victim herself was easily groomed with a potent mixture of treats and threats – it's a strange combination when you think about it. To terrify at the same time as entice seems like a contradiction in terms, like taking one step backwards for every step forwards. With children, though, it is a powerful mix that has the opposite effect; the two approaches strengthen each other. The child is desperate for the treat, desperate to please and be endorsed – and they are simultaneously desperate not to receive the content of the threat. Such desperation is powerful and compelling. For this girl, the treats amounted to crisps and sweets Mummy could not afford, and the threat went like this: 'If you tell Mummy about us she won't believe you – she really likes us, much more than she likes you. We'll find out you've told her, the treats will stop and you'll be punished which will hurt. If she does believe you – which she won't – she'll have to stop working and you'll have no money. It'll be your fault when you all starve and Mummy can't pay the rent and you live on the pavement forever.'

Mr and Mrs O abused their young victim for many weeks until they couldn't resist progressing the severity of the abuse to the point that they visibly injured the girl. Blood-stained clothing was spotted by Mum at bath time, and the police investigation began. The little girl was very clear in her video interview that Mrs O had been as fully involved in the abuse as her husband.

2. Ms P

Ms P was an able professional woman. She had been in a relationship with her partner for many years and they were soul-mates on every level except the intellectual one. She definitely had the brains, while he had the brawn, but I'm not knocking the combination; it seemed to work for them. Mr P had a history of sexual assaults and harassment pertaining to young teenage girls – he had pursued one of his victims so relentlessly that the family had been forced to leave the area and change their identity. Ms P had the opportunity to leave him at the point these offences were prosecuted, but she decided to disbelieve the complainant and stand by her man.

The pair came to our notice when we received intelligence from another police force that had examined a paedophile's computer and found emails containing indecent images of children that had been sent to him by Mr and Ms P. At first we presumed that Mr P was our offender and the initial warrant related only to him. Subsequent examination of their joint computer changed everything. They clearly had a 'colourful' sexual life, and were dipping their carnal toes in peculiar waters most people would not want to know existed. It was this discovery that first alerted me to consider Ms P's involvement; I reasoned that if they were so together in every other area of their private lives, it was possible that he did not have a secret 'child abuse' world from which she was excluded but actually shared his enjoyment of indecent images with her.

From further examination of the computer it was soon obvious that Ms P was working with Mr P in not only watching indecent images of children but also distributing pictures from their collection to other paedophiles worldwide. It was a part of their sexual life together that she had started off tolerating, progressed into assisting, and ended up relishing. One of the scariest aspects of Ms P was that her profession was a responsible role within a respected agency that would have required her to deal with victims and families of child sexual abuse on occasions. As part of the investigation we found that she seriously breached the mandatory privacy rules that were integral to her job. But scarier still: she never seemed to make the link as to why this was a worry.

She is now unemployed, a sad squandering of a very able woman.

3. Mrs Q

Mrs Q was a married woman with a large brood of children. Her husband was one of the worst child abusers I have ever encountered – he is the cruelty merchant I mentioned in Chapter 3 who was given the 'least sentence' by the judge for his tyrannical crimes. He actually succeeded in covering the whole gambit of child abuse during his time in the family home, and the children's decimation was his only legacy. The family lived in poverty, mainly because the significant amount of welfare money being poured into their home was frittered on alcohol and gambling before it ever reached the children. In fact I think it served only to fuel the immense suffering they endured because the richer mum and dad felt themselves, the drunker they became – and so, the more severely they dished out the abuse. Basics were luxuries, luxuries were unheard of, and squalor ruled the roost.

Mrs Q was a completely passive mother. She didn't stand up for anyone but herself. The critical lack of protection she offered her children constituted serious neglect, and she too had a chasm with two sides to choose from. Choosing his side meant she didn't get hurt, she was kept in alcohol and relinquished of any responsibility. Choosing the children's side would have risked personal assault, reined in the drinking, required personal effort, and possibly even led to his departure. For her own sake, it was better to have him there than not have him there – despite the fact that he was systematically destroying the children.

The sexual abuse was extensive. Mr Q could regularly be found in the bathroom with the eldest son and, despite the boy developing a strange obsession with bottoms and toilets, Mrs Q never challenged what it was they did in there for hours at a time. The babysitter they chose was a local man who frequently babysat alone. Mr and Mrs Q were well aware of his many criminal convictions for adult and child sexual abuse, and yet they still chose to give him unsupervised care of their young tribe at bedtime. He violated each one.

I think this next incident sums up Mrs Q's appalling approach to parenting. During one of many video interviews I held with her pre-teen daughter, the girl reported that she had had sex with a local lad. The episode had taken place in her bedroom one weekend and she reported that Mum had been downstairs throughout. I later spoke with Mrs Q and when I asked her if she had known what was taking place between the two children, she replied, 'Yes, I knew what was happening. But what was I supposed to do about it? I was getting my dinner.'

As far as I am aware, Mrs Q did not physically commit a sexual act against any of her children. However, she allowed them to be sexually abused by others on a regular basis solely because it served her needs not to disallow it – and so to my mind Mrs Q *did* sexually abuse her children. She was as guilty as the men who committed the acts.

Why?

I don't think you have to be a woman to find that an impossible question to answer. But, as a woman, if a child ran out in front of a lorry I would run out after them and put myself in its path; it would be an instinctive act of protection I would barely think about. In the animal kingdom, adult females fight to the death to protect their young and, in the human kingdom, we fight nearly as hard to protect everyone else's as well. In God's kingdom, we uphold the protection of children as paramount above all other considerations, including our own welfare – no, *especially* our own welfare. It is arguable that if our own welfare was more important than theirs we wouldn't give birth in the first place. It certainly didn't do much for my welfare at the time!

A woman's decision to choose the man's side of the chasm is based on a hideous dose of selfishness that would rather the children bore the consequences of her survival than she bore the consequences of their protection. I have found that once the fatal decision is reached, she renders herself willing for all the other paedophile characteristics to become her, *and they do*. Her tolerance of child sexual abuse becomes active enjoyment, her covering of his tracks becomes an inherent deviousness that shapes her life, and a need to control becomes as imperative to her survival as the original decision.

I want to clear up a few misunderstandings that may have arisen before I go any further. Firstly, when I say the 'man's side of the chasm', I am not referring to any man walking the street but solely to the paedophiles.

Only a paedophile would seek to excavate such a horrible chasm of choice. Secondly, the word 'survival' can have a plethora of connotations for women making the decision. For some it is mortal survival that presumes on personal violence if the child's side is chosen. For others it is financial or marital survival that would rather tolerate the child's abuse than the consequences of divorce. For yet others it is the survival of a relationship, a job, or even reputation that fires their decision.

- For Ms N it was the fear of suffering abuse herself and losing another partner. His violence tapped into a dank well of nastiness already in her.
- For Ms O it was the fear of her own children being abused that sent her over to Mr O's side, but the fact that she had always accepted that he was a paedophile means that in essence she had made her choice long before.
- For Ms P it was the fear of being excluded from a part of Mr P's life and potentially losing him. Their relationship was a closed shop between the two of them that had lost perspective and, once her decision was made, she joined him happily. From her vantage point on his side of the chasm she acquired a distorted view of everything else around her.
- For Mrs Q it was the fear of having to take responsibility and losing the addictions on which she leant so heavily. She was like a child herself in her dependency on Mr Q, almost to the point of being in awe of him and, no matter how severe the destruction of her children, she was more likely to ignore the abuse than protect them.

Once these women chose to stand on the man's side of the chasm, they slipped down the abusive slope with him and became paedophiles in their own right, unequivocally. None of their situations condone their decisions; they were all entirely responsible for the child sexual abuse they either perpetrated or permitted. Let me make this absolutely clear. I am not saying that the woman's decision to choose the man's side of the chasm makes it *his* fault that *she* offends. Making a choice does not bring exoneration; it carries equal responsibility. For right-minded women the paedophile's side is more unthinkable than death itself. As an example of choosing sides, let's look at the case of Mrs R.

Mrs R

I met Mrs R on uniformed patrol when the radio despatched me to a violent domestic dispute taking place in the upmarket end of town. Like paedophilia, domestic violence is socially universal – indeed one of the reasons we execute our paedophile warrants so early in the morning is to catch the overwhelming number of our customers who head off for high-powered jobs first thing. If child sexual abuse was merely the domain of alcoholic vagrants wearing long brown macs we could hang on till lunchtime and have a lie-in ourselves. So it is with domestic violence – bullies are bullies whether they wear an executive suit, tattered overalls, a robe or a uniform.

For all that Mr R was highly regarded in his field as a leading academic, to his family he was just a common bully. Mrs R had suffered greatly at his violent hands for years, and frequently placed herself between him and the children when she believed they were in the firing line of his explosive temper. She felt paralysed to prevent the emotional battering they took in that household, but

their physical one she stoically shouldered, often literally. On the day police were finally called, Mr R had
taken a hockey stick to his wife and daughter. Mrs R
had borne the brunt of the assault as usual, but the stick
had connected with the daughter a few times, causing
nearly as much injury as distress. That swung the pen-
dulum for Mrs R and the grief-stricken woman rang 999.
You know the old adage about bullies being cowards?
Well, when we got to the house we found this monster –
you know, the big brave man who had pounded his wife
for years and just laid into his little girl with a hockey
stick – yes, we found *this* monster locked in the bathroom
cowering under the sink where the nasty police wouldn't
catch him. We kicked the door down and there he was,
whimpering for mercy. (He didn't get any.)

Mrs R chose her children's side of the chasm at great
cost to herself. She bore the violence of her husband –
often on their behalf – and on the first occasion he overrode that decision and pounded them anyway she
risked her own survival and rang the police. She was
genuinely terrified for her life when she picked up the
phone – he had always threatened to kill her if she
reported him – *but the children were paramount.* She had to
remain on their side of the chasm, no matter what it cost
her.

OK, so Mr R wasn't a paedophile and we're majoring
on child sexual abuse – let's consider Mrs S then.

The case of Mrs S

For years, Mrs S had tolerated her husband's use of
pornography. She had never liked its place in their marriage, but had permitted it. Why? For the reasons he said
it was necessary. She occasionally joined in watching it

because it was so important to him. Their adult children had flown the nest and were producing grandchildren at an impressive rate. One evening, Mr S cajoled Mrs S into agreeing to view some Internet pornography with him and, as the session unfolded he introduced indecent images of children onto the screen. She was horror-struck. The images were as awful as the realization that he was well-versed in where to find them. Her panic flashed her little grandchildren before her eyes in a rap-idly moving slide show that interjected memories of their own children as youngsters. Into this vortex of panic poured the images of the poor little mites whose suffering her husband had not only enjoyed himself but expected *her* to be gratified by. She could not think of a greater slur on her character.

Their marriage ended that night. It wasn't just the realization that she didn't know her husband; it was the appalling realization that he didn't know her. She chose the children's side of the chasm – her children, her chil-dren's children and all the unknown children whose abuse she had witnessed. The following day she rang the police while he was at work and gave us his com-puters, even rummaging through the garage for an old one. In the last conversation I had with her she was still agonizing over whether he could possibly have inter-fered with their own children: How did she broach such a question with them? Could she cope with the answer? Was it best left now? How could she tell them about his arrest? What about the grandchildren?

Close contacts

Incidentally, when paedophiles are arrested and placed on police bail, the parents of any children they come into close contact with are informed, as are employers if their job is child-related in any form. Families, marriages, careers, reputations, mortgages, friendships . . . the arrest can blow a bomb through them all. This action usually comes as a shock to offenders, particularly those watching Internet images, who reason that they haven't actually touched a child so what's the problem? They are unconvicted at this point and presume on the Data Protection Act upholding their right to privacy, but the law safeguards children first and rightly so. When offenders are watching indecent images the consequences of capture do not fully register, though by their own admission it wouldn't make much difference if it did. I recently dealt with a very dapper guy whose job included a role in the sale of children's clothing on the high street. He didn't actually connect with children as part of this, but his role was deemed to place him too close to little ones for comfort and his employer was informed. He was dismissed.

The exception

Through my job I have seen thousands of indecent images of children. If I was to make a rough estimate I would say that about 10 per cent of those images have portrayed a woman in the abuse. Some are pinning the child down to assist a male offender and others are more fully committing sexual acts with the children. There is no distinction between the age and gender of children they defile and, while I have never seen the women subjected to force themselves, I have frequently seen them treating children with violence. Yes, grown women who have not been moved by the agonized pleas of tiny innocents begging for the pain to stop; these women have carried on inflicting whatever it is they are doing, even been goaded on by the anguish of the child they are hurting. I find such images among the hardest to watch.

Earlier, I mentioned an exceptional case. All the paedophiles I have dealt with have been male or, rarely, a female operating in conjunction with a man. I have never come across a situation where a paedophile woman has been executing offences while in a relationship with a non-offending man. I'm not saying such a woman isn't out there – I have just never met or heard of her.

Mrs T was highly unusual because she was a female paedophile operating alone and solely for her own pleasure. She was dealt with by a colleague and we all agreed that we had never come across such a specimen before. Can you imagine a group of entomologists clad in baggy trousers and teensy binoculars hunting among the bracken on the moors when they suddenly discover a new and more startling species of insect than they had ever found before? We were like that in the office when this case came to light.

Mrs T was a single woman with grown-up children, one of whom was expecting the first grandchild. To all intents and purposes she was completely ordinary: she ate muesli every morning, she wore tights under her jeans, and she was making the big 'Do I or don't I?' decision about HRT. I don't actually remember how her offences were revealed, but I do recall that we were all particularly disturbed by the images she was watching. Her penchant was for particularly young children, babies and toddlers, and the abuse she enjoyed watching was severe indeed, causing extreme distress and harm to the children depicted. Augmenting these images was a collection of child abuse stories she had downloaded from the Internet and was reading alongside her cookery magazine about how to make bread pudding. Such abusive stories are commonplace and entirely legal, but they're dreadful to read. I don't know how, but sometimes they feel as bad watching the images; they express abuse in the most graphic and blood-curdling of terms that leave your imagination trawling through the cesspit with the author. I hate reading them and have developed a way of scanning the pages to glean their gist but not lodge the detail in my brain. Having to look at illegal material is a requirement of my job – having to digest what I can't prosecute anyway is not on my agenda.

We were so surprised by Mrs T we had to ask ourselves if there was actually a man lurking somewhere in the murky world behind her smart front door. Once we had ruled this scenario out we moved on to wondering if she was dealing in child sexual abuse for financial gain. Maybe she was selling images or even blackmailing other paedophiles who had crawled out from their apparently respectable stones at the same inopportune moment that she crawled out from hers. No, that investigation proved to be a dead end too. As she herself later endorsed, she was addicted to violent indecent images of young children for the sexual gratification it brought her – nothing more and nothing less.

The compassion I felt for my colleague who had to tell her grown-up daughter that Granny could not have contact with the new baby because Granny was a dangerous paedophile was dwarfed only by the compassion I felt for the daughter upon hearing such news. I reckon there can be nothing worse than finding out your mum is a paedophile.

You couldn't make it up

Do you remember little Janie from earlier in this chapter? When her attack was reported she went to live with her grandmother. The woman had not a penny to her name, but what she lacked in the bank she made up for in her heart and her pledge to care for Janie was a great outcome for the child.

Shortly after Ms N and her boyfriend were sent to prison, the grandmother asked me to visit and help explain some of the legal processes that were still ongoing. While she was putting the kettle on I sat with Janie in the lounge area of the house and the little girl made a derogatory remark about herself. I was shocked to hear a child so young put herself down in this way and looking her fully in the face I countered, 'No, Janie, that's not true. You're lovely and you mustn't ever forget it.'

A few months later I was passing the house and popped in again. Ms N was due out of prison and I wanted to clarify that all protective measures were understood by the grandmother and in place. As part of our chat she went off to find some papers she wanted to show me, leaving me alone with Janie. I couldn't resist asking the question I most wanted answered.

'Janie, have you remembered what I said to you?'

Her face broke into a winning smile and beaming brightly she replied, 'Yes, you said I'm lovely.'

That moment is one of the highlights of my police career.

8

What the Paedophiles Say . . . And What the Children Say

What the paedophiles say

One Saturday morning, when I was about twelve years old, my sister Alice was having her piano lesson from Mum in the other room. This conveniently meant that Mum was safely out of the way: the noise of the piano coupled with the closed door and high level of concentration resulted in a nicely distracted parent for the lesson's duration. The night before this particular Saturday, Mum had made a batch of chocolate brownies which were an extremely special creation. She didn't make them very often so they were a wonderful treat when they appeared, and we were only ever allowed one at teatime: strictly *one* and absolutely no chance of extending the ration by the merest crumb. Each mouthful of my chosen brownie – always spent a while sizing them up to make sure I got the biggest – was a gourmet delight to be savoured. You're probably getting where this story is going, aren't you?

Yes, on the Saturday in question I reckoned that Mum was safely ensconced teaching Alice and it was worth risking all to nick a brownie from the fridge. My timing could not have been worse. I was tucking into my second bite, still standing there by the open fridge door, when Mum came into the kitchen to get a pencil. She stopped in her tracks when she saw me. What now? My racing mind churned over a few possible responses to her rather pointless question, 'And what *do* you think you're doing?'

- 'I just wanted some raw broccoli to nibble on and when I opened the fridge this wretched brownie jumped into my hand.'
- 'I'm about to spring clean the house, do the big shop, empty the loft, landscape the garden and tarmac the drive, so I thought an energy boost might come in handy.'
- 'I saw some toxic mould growing on this brownie and couldn't bear for any of you to eat it and contract salmonella so I thought I'd have it. Oh, it's OK, you don't have to thank me.'
- 'I know Alice hasn't done any practice this week and thought I'd support her in the doghouse. I'm nice like that, and it's not my fault, I had to think of a very naughty thing to match just how awfully lazy she's been.'
- 'I heard on the news that girls of my age need to eat a chocolate brownie at exactly nine minutes and thirty-seven seconds past ten on a Saturday morning otherwise they become susceptible to life-threatening ulcers. It's purely for medicinal purposes, and if you keep the fridge door open while you eat, the cool breeze helps to blow the infection even further away.'

As it was I didn't say very much – largely because there wasn't very much to say. My horrified silence and guilt-ridden face told Mum all she needed to know without me opening my mouth, which I couldn't do anyway because it was packed with brownie I was trying to swallow without her noticing. (I'm not sure why I attempted this when I was clearly eating it. Even at that doomed stage I was trying to hide the truth!)

However, if chocolate brownies could speak for themselves, the part-eaten delicacy would have told a different story: 'I was sitting here passing the time with my mates when suddenly the fridge door opened and a great light shone over the shelves. The lid of our box was lifted away which made the light even brighter for a moment until it was slowly clouded out by a large hand. Darkness fell. The hand hovered over my mates for a while – backwards and forwards – then the next thing I knew it pinched me really hard at the sides, whisked me up, up, up . . . and, from nowhere, two sharp fangs sunk deep into my back and I haven't seen my hindquarters since.'

When paedophiles are caught by the police it is that chocolate brownie moment. More often than not they are glaringly in the frame for the offences they have committed: they either own the computer containing indecent images, they have been identified through email and mobile phone details, or a child has specifically named them as the abuser. (Because most offenders are known to their victims, they are easily named.) And also, like that chocolate brownie moment, there is no resemblance between the account of the hunter and the account of his prey. Analysing what paedophiles say to defend themselves could fill a library of books in itself and we've got one chapter, so I've written a summary of basics that is not intended to plough the whole field of the subject but just weed out a few examples.

I don't have much respect for the defences that child sex offenders hide behind; constructing believable excuses for why you have been determinedly harming young innocents is no mean feat. The offence is so extensive in its severity and consequences that the defence needs to be equally mammoth to stand a chance of obscuring the truth. The account a paedophile will contrive tends to fall into one of two brackets – it is either one the police have heard a thousand times, or he pitches his imagination against his dilemma and concocts a new and wholly incredible story. I groan at the familiar ones – they are as old as the hills – and I groan louder at the new ones because they are usually that bit more bizarre. I am quite sure that I would not make a very good defence barrister. Besides not being able to live with myself if I found hooks for guilty people to hang acquittals on, I could not keep a straight face when trying to convince a courtroom of people to believe a load of contrived nonsense.

There are lots of obvious reasons why paedophiles create defences to deflect their responsibility for violating children. Beneath these obvious reasons lurk two not-so-obvious ones which are significant, and when we've looked at them we'll take a look at some true defences I have heard.

Not-so-obvious reason number 1

As with all criminals who have to account for their crimes, paedophiles want to deceive everyone into thinking that they are not blameworthy. I don't suppose I'll win any awards for that observation. They want the police and the courts, their families, neighbours, friends and employers to disbelieve the accusation. Many other criminals don't carry the full weight of this burden – plenty of folk in their circle already know they are a burglar or a drug addict and the list of people to be deceived is reduced accordingly. But where I have found that paedophiles most differ from other offenders is that the person they principally deceive is themselves. When they deny the abuse, they are drowning in monumental *self*-denial.

Your average burglar knows that when he jemmies open your patio doors, disconnects your plasma telly and waltzes off with your car keys he is committing the offence of burglary. He easily dismisses the anguish he is causing to you, but he would be the first to admit to himself that he is a burglar – it's almost a chosen career path. (Not many do it sporadically – it's too lucrative and the system too lenient to waste time resisting its ill-gotten gains.) A paedophile does not think the same way.

He distorts what he has done to the point that it becomes acceptable to him. It is a process he begins *before* he abuses, not after he's been caught. He doesn't turn into an active paedophile overnight; from the point he is first aware of his sexual attraction to children, he starts building a mental wall that is near completion as he begins offending. There's a whole compendium of mind games to be played out. Each game he conquers adds a brick to the wall: tussles about conscience, evasion, opportunity, understanding, obsession, tactics, delusion, lifestyle, reputation, sexuality, denial, self-persuasion. Once the wall is sufficiently cemented he can progress into physically acting on what he has long been thinking about . . . and not many offenders come to notice at the first offence. Detection usually takes years and, throughout those years, the building process continues and the mental wall gets higher. By the time the police have caught up with him – *if* they catch up with him – and are demanding he accounts for his behaviour, he has concreted his years of excuses and dismissals into an indestructible wall that prevents any other reasoning from getting through. In fact, non-abusers become the outsiders for existing on the other side of the wall and not comprehending why it's acceptable to defile children. That's when the construction is complete. There is no storm or missile that can damage the formidable wall now encasing the workings of his mind.

Not-so-obvious reason number 2

Most criminals want to avoid arrest and imprisonment at all costs. I won't win any awards for that observation either. Paedophiles also want to avoid arrest and imprisonment at all costs, but they have an extra cost that is so dear to them they cannot afford to pay it – when they are captured they cannot indulge their sexual attraction to children. Their computer is seized, their imperative secrecy is blown, their involvement with the child is terminated, their on-line access to like-minded contacts ceases . . . and all too rarely a few of them are incarcerated in the clink. Maintaining the freedom to abuse is the overriding reason why they must evade detection.

But going to prison doesn't completely halt their offending. In jail, child sex offenders are segregated from other prisoners for their own safety. Do we think they sit and chat about the weather all day? 'No, Rebecca, of course we don't!' They share their fantasies and forge links on which to capitalize outside; such closeting together can *strengthen* offenders to resist the rehabilitation and punishment imprisonment is designed to deliver. Detaining paedophiles together can actually *furnish* abuse. Personally I think they should be kept apart and prevented from befriending each other – the protection of children is supposed to be paramount to the comfort of prisoners. It's a hard irony that the prison system offers paedophiles a higher level of protection than society offers children. In prison sex offenders are guaranteed by law to enjoy the same precious safety that they annihilate in their victims. If segregation in prison was abolished I expect that sex offenders would protest on the basis of their human right to protection from attack – yet they are in prison, requiring it because they have slaughtered that same human right in a child.

You know, it makes me wonder. One of the things many paedophiles love about abusing children is the power and control involved; they relish the intimidation and terror side of it all. But they themselves don't actually enjoy being bullied and scared in prison. You would think that that oppressive environment is just the kind of thing they would savour, but amazingly they are not gratified by violence from someone bigger and stronger when *they are* the one who is smaller and weaker. Odd, isn't it, how abuse seems so outrageous to them when they find themselves the victim.

True defences

The two distinct areas of child abusers I have worked among – those watching indecent images and those committing abuse in person – produce two distinct catalogues of defences, but one defence is common to both. It heads up the list entitled 'One That Police Have Heard A Thousand Times' and is arguably the most contentious, for some would say it has an element of merit. But I do not concur with that school of thought.

The most common defence I have heard to committing child sexual abuse is that the offender was abused as a child. *This is not a defence in law – it carries no weight in the statute books; it isn't mentioned.* However, the court process sometimes operates as though it was an acceptable explanation. Do you remember how comprehensively Mr G's eleventh-hour memory of childhood abuse interrupted his sentencing in Chapter 3? I can't think of anything else he could have said that would have had such an invasive and costly effect on proceedings.

The assumption that this is a fair defence is an insult to the overwhelming majority of child sexual abuse survivors who do not grow into adults that harm children. It does not follow that if you were abused as a child you become a child abuser. I have spoken to many adults abused as children who are not abusers; in fact, only a tiny number I have spoken with have grown into offenders. If this defence had any substance at all I would not have had those conversations. Child abuse survivors know the nightmare of abuse better than anyone, and the ones I have met seek to steer away from it, not channel their lives into it. One woman who suffered extensive sexual abuse at the hands of her father and brother grew up to be an exceptional mother to her own four children and lots of other needy youngsters she fostered. She was an example of motherhood to which most women would aspire.

In my opinion, where an abused child has grown into an abuser, his history does not mitigate his crime. It may have contributed to the sexual attraction to children *in his mind* but it does not diminish his responsibility for acting on it. The offences he commits are still fully committed – being abused as a child does not make an abuser some kind of partial offender who commits partial offences for which he is partially accountable. To the victim they are a violator, arguably more so, because this violator knows how terrible violation feels and yet still determines to violate.

This defence suggests that abusers who were abused are thrown into their offending like a piece of victimized jetsam abandoned to the mercy of an abusive current they cannot stand against. That would make them distinctive from other paedophiles because it would mark them out as helpless, weakened, beyond awareness, without a grip on their life: 'Poor old thing, he couldn't help it, it wasn't his fault; after all that happened to him there was nothing he could do.' BUT – and it's a big 'BUT' – the evidence says otherwise. I have seen no difference in the tenacity and ruthlessness shown by abusers who were abused and abusers who were not. If the former really were helpless in some way it would show. Not a bit of it. They display the same paedophile characteristics of being in vicious control and behaving with precise and well-planned deviousness; they know exactly what they're doing and they determine to do it. They are no longer the hunted, they are the hunter. If anything, they can make for a more callous hunter because their painful memories of being the hunted hack a fierce edge of revenge and punishment into their crimes.

I fervently believe in (and long for) a justice system that promotes the safety of children as paramount. The proportion of paedophiles who were abused as a child have my sympathy for their own experience of suffering and they remain entitled to the relevant help as long as they live – but their suffering does not reduce the agony they perpetrate later in life. I think the law should deal with them as severely as any other sex offender, for their crimes are as severe as any other sex offender. An identified predator is an absolute danger irrespective of why he is that way and, while being abused himself may be a factor in why he has become dangerous, it is not a permit to commit offences.

For any child protection professionals reading this there is another side to the proffered 'I was abused = I am an abuser' equation we can't ignore if it has merit. If the equation is valid it represents a key to intercepting future offenders. Victims could be identified as probable abusers, and we could work with them in that vein to diminish the number of paedophiles developing among us. Of course we don't take such an obscene and blanket approach towards victims because (among other things) it would be entirely groundless. The whole equation just isn't that simple, it's not that scientific, not that quantifiable, not that probable, not that inevitable, not even that common. The equation does not equate on any other level, so it does not equate to a defence. To uphold the protection of future children as paramount we would be obliged to treat victims differently if it did.

Every paedophile has his own personal reasons as to why he offends: none of them excuse, justify or exonerate him. Absolutely nothing has any merit as a permit to decimate children.

The Internet defences

Firstly we'll take a look at some of the most frequent defences used by Internet offenders who are arrested for watching indecent images of children. The police have just hammered on their door at an unearthly hour and they are horrified to find themselves in the chocolate brownie moment of capture. What do they say now? The things they come out with make little sense to me. Considering that paedophiles generally offend for years before they're caught, you'd think they'd have time to come up with something a bit more substantial. Put it this way: if there was a viable defence to the crime I reckon someone would have thought of it by now – enough intelligent people have tried – so it reminds me that there obviously isn't. This is what prisoners most commonly say when we interview them:

1. I was hunting for adult pornography when all these child images downloaded into my computer.
2. I am depressed.
3. I was curious to see what indecent images of children look like.

Let's answer them.

1. Child images do not download from adult pornography websites – they download from child ones. The makers of adult pornography are keen to ensure their sites remain legal and their income afloat, therefore they are careful to ensure that children do not feature in their material. That means an offender has to choose to be in a child site to see a child image, then he has to choose to download it, then he has to choose to look at the next one and the next one after that. Then he has to choose to do it all again tomorrow. If he only wants adult material he will ignore any child links that appear, and he will certainly never explore or revisit a child website he has inadvertently entered. If you want to buy a chair you don't browse in websites selling freezers, and if you inadvertently find yourself looking at freezers you log off and enter different search terms to ensure you access chairs. People who hunt for adult material get adult material; people who hunt for children get children.
2. Most of us experience depression at some point in life and I do not see what it has got to do with watching indecent images of children. This is such an inadequate defence it is hardly worth wasting ink on. The chemical imbalances linked to depression do not reprogramme people into becoming sexually attracted to children, and they do not make them enjoy indecent images that they used to abhor and would never

have dreamed of viewing before they were ill. The depression argument has no foundation or credibility; being depressed is not a defence to being a paedophile.

3. I cannot imagine such curiosity overcoming a right-minded person. You have to be heading for the wrong side of perverted to wonder what it looks like when a child is raped. Mere curiosity does not explain the thunderous leap into unlawful and reviled territory that an Internet offender takes when he views indecent images of children. If it is possible to put the victims aside for a moment, the action itself is a serious criminal offence with devastating consequences. Who takes a risk like that because they are feeling a bit nosey? (I am inquisitive about what it feels like to steal £10 million and live like an heiress, but the illegality deters me and I manage to overcome.) Of course, the thunderous leap is taken by offenders because the deterrent is not strong enough to prevent it; the curiosity is not just a passing interest at all but a powerful drive, a burgeoning sexual attraction to children that will risk anything, everything to be fed. Apart from sounding suspiciously like a brick in the mind-games wall, the 'curiosity' defence is simply far too weak for the power of the crime.

Regardless of what anyone might say to counter these defences, the offender's computer has the final word. If a suspect is really just looking for adult pictures, or is clinically depressed or feeling a tad curious they will discover child images once. They will be distraught at the horror they see and never *ever* want to go near them again. (And boy, watch them jump out their skin next time there's a knock at the door!) But Internet offenders don't look once – they look repeatedly, for weeks and months and years. The computer shows *beyond question* how many times an offender has gone back for more: the singular visits to child sites that would support the defences transpire to be an established pattern of behaviour that rebuts them. These people know and love what they do, over and over again; their defences hold no water and it's the repetition that pulls the plug. Curiosity indeed! If the legal system paid deference to people who are only curious about their crime and not actually meaning to break the law, where would we all be? I'd be in a tax haven on a Caribbean island, I don't know about you.

The 'In person' defences
Now let's look at what sex offenders who abuse children in person most commonly say:

1. The child coerced me; I didn't really want to be sexual with them.
2. The child is lying.
3. I have an unhappy home life/marriage.

I think we can answer them too.

1. We covered this issue in Chapter 1, but a quick recap will tell us that a child cannot consent to sexual activity in law, therefore whoever instigated the activity *it is always illegal*. The defence is void from the outset because the actions and history of the child are irrelevant and the adult is always responsible. Also, it is incredibly rare for a child to be so sexually confident that they seek to seduce an adult, so statistically it should be an incredibly rare defence, not a very common one. And we know that if a child is displaying such unnatural behaviour it is indicative of them having

already been badly misused and deserving extra care, not extra harm. It is pathetic beyond words for an adult to believe they are not guilty of paedophilia if they capitulate to a child's sexual invitation. Without excuse they take gross advantage of that child's brokenness and are indisputably a paedophile. The sole disparity between them and an offender who has worked hard to groom their victim is that it was all too tragically easy for the former. The only mitigation I can imagine is in a scenario where a teenager has presented as a convincing adult, and the adult has genuinely believed and wanted them to be so.

2. To say 'The child is lying' is a very lazy defence and I generally take it as a veiled admission of guilt. I reason that if the bloke had anything better to claim he would claim it, so clearly he is out of excuses and scraping the barrel. Sadly, though, it can be as incisive a defence as it is lazy because the victim's truthfulness is at the heart of proving most sexual offences. Of course truthfulness must be an absolute requirement, but nip down to your local Crown Court next time you have a few spare hours and you'll see what I'm lamenting. Compelling evidence like witness accounts and forensic matches can count for little if the defence barrister finds room for manoeuvre in the victim's testimony. That manoeuvre may only amount to confusion or distress, it doesn't actually have to amount to falsehood, but if the victim can be brought into question on any level – however cheap – then they can be classed as 'brought into question' and discredited. Some don't even realize it's happened. They walk away from the courtroom in dazed realization that the barrister has wiped the floor with them and ask a bewildered, 'What did I do wrong?' Picture the scene: they are standing numb and trembling in the

witness box – terrified, crying and embarrassed – pitched against a strutting barrister who is confident, sharp and aggressive. The victim is there for the taking. It's like watching a hound with his quarry. It is not difficult for the doziest of lawyers to weaken the strongest of witnesses when they are so vulnerable, and that's why so many victims complain that going to court is like being raped again.

'The child is lying' defence has a particularly cruel and exploitative dimension. It goes like this: an abused child is a damaged child; a damaged child can display unseemly behaviour because of the damage inflicted; children displaying unseemly behaviour are easily dismissed as unreliable. Too many times I have heard legal personnel make comments like this: 'You can't put that lad in the witness box. He's far too contrary; his behaviour is all over the place. It's much too risky to proceed with him the way he is. The defence will make mincemeat of him. He doesn't present as a very good witness at all. Who knows what he'll do?'

It's a double whammy, a final twisting of the knife, a nasty catch-22 the child is powerless to overcome. The abuse that defects their behaviour is the abuse that negates their integrity because they are defectively behaved. So they are not allowed to tell about the damage because they are deemed too damaged to tell it believably – and that decision is taken by the prosecuting bodies. Heaven help those children when the people who are supposed to be on their side sit in such crippling judgement of them. Surely poor behaviour is part of the evidence that proves the point.

But *defendant* truthfulness doesn't seem so highly valued or potent to court business . . . strange old places, courtrooms, aren't they? I sometimes wonder if that's why the characters inside them dress up in wigs and robes and tights and things, you know, to remind us that this is primarily a theatre detached from reality, where feelings are not genuinely felt, and events are stage-managed beyond veracity. I'd like to see court personnel wearing rugby strips to demonstrate that the courtroom is an uncompromising place that does not tolerate pretence, where fairness dictates proceedings on a level playing field, where no one is acting or driven by selfish gain, where a team works together with integrity towards honourable goals and the rules are the same for both sides.

Very few children lie about sexual abuse. Think about it. When the complaint is made, their life is turned upside down. They are interviewed by police in great detail – we don't settle for 'He raped me' (or a child's equivalent); we require the absolute detail of every physical action that constitutes the claim. That's a lot to invent and then remember for months if you're lying. An extensive fallout reverberates around everyone involved, intrusive medical examinations are undertaken, the daily routine is overhauled to prevent a recurrence, freedom is lost: 'You're not going out like that any more'/'You can't go and play at their house again'/'No more violin, swimming, horse-riding lessons for you after what that teacher did' and so on. And *that's* before we've asked how the child knew so much about sex to make the lies up in the first place, and that's before we have analysed the truth of the circumstances surrounding the claim. We know the hallmarks of an authentic account and the cracks will soon appear in a story that is not ringing true. It is difficult enough for a child to persevere with the legal system when their testimony is factual – it borders on the impossible when it is a pack of lies. I'm not saying that no child has ever lied; I'm saying it's very rare, particularly when you compare it to how commonly the defence is used.

(I'm putting my head on the block here, but I must admit that I have found teenage girls to be the group of children most likely to fabricate a story, and usually in relation to a man in authority a girl feels passionate about – either passionate resentment or passionate attraction. She is old enough to know the power of her scheming, wise enough to know some sexual facts, and charged enough by her hormones to go through with it. Sometimes – and only sometimes – teenage girls need their accounts to be particularly authenticated, but that is the responsibility of the police and the CPS. It need not destroy lives if the job is done with proper care and sensitivity.)

3. Finally: 'It wasn't my fault I sexually assaulted the child, I have an unhappy home life and my marriage is on the rocks.' When this defence is wheeled out I always want to shake my head and ask the offender, 'Your point being?' Good grief, if sad home lives and rocky marriages led to paedophilia the electoral roll could virtually double as the Sex Offender's Register. It is no defence whatsoever; it amounts to no more than a whine. We all pass through times when home life is unhappier than we want it to be; for some people this is a more severe experience than others, but the notion that it breeds a sexual attraction to children that mitigates defiling them is nonsense. Unhappy home lives are sorry places – from systematic violence to occasional rows – but they are nothing to do with being sexually aroused by children. Occasionally John and I argue; occasionally we have bad days at work that we bring home; occasionally the children are more infuriating than trying to ring the bank; occasionally all these things happen on the same day. They

are unhappy days. I can categorically state that neither of us walks away from a heated exchange, steams
about the other one for being wrong *again* and then
thinks about abusing a child. It states the obvious to
say that you have to be paedophile to want to abuse a
child, whether your wife burnt the chicken or not.

New and incredible defences

Having covered the old and weary defences I thought
I'd share some from the 'new and wholly incredible' category. These are all defences recently offered to our Unit
by offenders who were prosecuted for possessing indecent images of children on their computers.

During his tape-recorded interview, Mr G presented
four excuses to his predicament that became progressively weaker as they became progressively novel.
Firstly, he claimed that he had never seen any indecent
images of children on his computer – having earlier stated that he spent hours a day using it. I tell you the
machine was full of child material of all levels; a donkey
could have logged on and found it in an instant. It was
not viable to believe that Mr G had never come across
the images and this dismissive approach was the line I
took with him. He changed tack. His second excuse was,
'Ah, you're talking about that computer, that silver one
from the drawing room? Oh, why didn't you say so? I've
got it now; you see, that one's not mine, it belongs to an
unknown man who left it with me yesterday for repair.'

I sat quietly for a moment, trying to imagine the
encounter. Personally I have never opened my front
door and found a complete stranger standing there who
gives me their computer and says, 'I'm not going to tell
you who I am or where I live, but please will you mend
my computer? I don't know if you know anything about
computers and I'm not going to tell you what's wrong

with it, but I will return next week to collect it.' The post-man calls sometimes, and the occasional Jehovah's Witness, but not any passers-by who have mistaken our humble abode for PC World.

Despite the sheer implausibility of it, this story was easily refuted by photographs of Mr G in the computer that undoubtedly connected him to it, and also a set of images downloaded just before we arrived on the day of his arrest – i.e. images accessed *after* the unknown man had supposedly handed his machine over. Mr G changed tack again and produced his third excuse.

'Well, OK, so I do own that computer; yes, the silver one from the drawing room, but I've only just bought it from a car boot sale, so the indecent material must have belonged to the previous owner.'

But Mr G's images were carefully filed in documents with his full name on and they dated back years, long before the fateful car boot sale. It was time to re-don the busy thinking cap and guess what happened next? Yes, Mr G changed tack again, and came up with excuse number four. I must give him credit where it's due: this one was worth waiting for.

'I only like flat-chested women and, in looking for such images on the computer, I must have downloaded younger women than I should have. I do apologize. How very reckless of me.'

I pulled a face, scratched my head and said, 'But that doesn't explain the toddlers and younger girls, it *cert-ainly* doesn't explain the boys, and it doesn't explain why your girlfriend is well-developed.'

At that point he jumped up and screamed at us all and the interview had to be terminated.

Mr B, the doctor, mentioned at the close of Chapter 1, presented a better thought-out defence than Mr G ever managed to come up with. Among other excuses for other offences, Mr B claimed to be undertaking a regrettable but helpful public service in distributing indecent images of children to fellow paedophiles. With a pained expression and thoughtful sighs – some longer than others for dramatic effect – he explained that if he hadn't done the 'valiant' thing of furnishing these offenders with indecent images they could have gone out and abducted a child to fulfil their perversions. Oh, he really didn't want to do what he did and hated the awfulness of it, but out of the kindness of his heart he risked everything to be a pillar of the community and prevent child abduction on a massive scale. What a guy! I can hear Samson himself wailing from here: 'Give me strength!'

Or how about the bloke who blamed local farmers for his plight? He even got his wife to write to the court and endorse his claim that pesticides recently sprayed on nearby crops had pickled his brain and made him download indecent images of children. I hope I don't need to spend time launching a torpedo at this particular defence. But I'd like to say to any farmers out there, please don't lose sleep over your crop-spraying habits, will you? I really don't think you have too much to worry about in terms of child protection and I'd hate you to get a complex.

That's what the paedophiles say. Now let's look at what the children say the paedophiles say; they know the truth better than anyone. They are the only ones who *really* know what the paedophiles say.

What the children say

The children describe the indescribable detail of their abuse and they say things like this:

- He hurt me.
- He scared me.
- He wouldn't stop.
- He was horrible.
- He made me cry.
- He made me bleed.
- He wouldn't listen to me.
- He made me do it.
- He said Mummy would be cross with me.
- He was stronger than me.
- He said no one would believe me.
- He said I'd be in trouble.
- He held me down, I couldn't get away.
- He said I had to else he'd hit me.
- He gave me posh things.
- He said no one else loved me.
- He said it would make me nicer.
- He told me to be brave.
- He said everyone does it.
- He said it was our special secret.
- He said we would both suffer if I told.
- He said that if I ever hide from him he'll find me.

They don't say that he was a nice man whose company they looked forward to keeping. They don't say the poor guy was depressed and needed cheering up. They don't say that he kept refusing their childish advances before reluctantly giving in. They don't say *they* made *him* do it. They don't say he only liked adults and the whole thing was an accident he didn't really mean. They don't say his wife didn't understand him. They don't say he didn't know what he was doing. They don't say it was all fine and they liked what happened. They don't plead for the man to be spared so the encounters can continue. They *do* sometimes ask if the threats of violence and rejection are going to be carried out now that they've told.

What the paedophiles say and what the children say the paedophiles say do not correlate. Both are talking about the same incidents and relationships yet they paint entirely different pictures. Who is lying? To my mind the discrepancy lies squarely in the paedophiles' corner for they are giving the police wildly contrasting explanations to the stories they are telling the children.

For a highly complex subject, the bedrock is actually very simple. Whatever the cause of their perversion and whatever they say about it, *paedophiles sexually abuse children because they want to*.

You couldn't make it up

What paedophiles say will never cease to amaze me. Last year I dealt with a man who was using the Internet to answer a whole variety of strange sexual questions he and his partner were posing. They were the kind of questions that most people are not capable of asking, and those who did enquire about such risqué territory would bitterly regret doing so the moment they received the answer.

One question this man and his partner were asking was how explicitly they could rocket the detail of their sexual life into cyberspace for to the rest of the world to see. Unfortunately for us, when we analysed their computer we found the answer to that question was 'as explicitly as you like'. We discovered that the pair had spared their camera lens absolutely nothing at all in what they had photographed and the angles at which they had done so. Once their private moments which should never have been made public were captured on film they uploaded the snapshots onto the Internet for anyone who may want to see them. (What a national tragedy that anyone may want to.)

It was relevant during the man's tape-recorded interview to ask him about the sexual pictures he and his partner were sharing with the world. He explained the nature of the photos in stomach-churning detail, and then he explained why they had been taken.

'We like to send them to our friends.'

We like to send Christmas cards to ours.

9.

The Case that Says it All

During my short reign as child protection co-ordinator at our church, I was involved in a protracted child sexual abuse case that reverberated around the membership. The actual offences had taken place years before and, much as the child had tried valiantly to suppress his devastation as he grew into adulthood, the trauma hadn't gone away. The pain of his suffering had gnawed relentlessly inside him, and I guess it was only ever a matter of time until it ground against the core of his being with such abrasion it could no longer be contained. When he was a young man his secret childhood pain exploded outwards over the family dynamics and beyond. The fallout was shocking; especially shocking because it did not fall out as he expected.

The whole story covers a period of many years, but the explosion itself occurred just before I began working in the Paedophile Unit, and just after I had implemented a thorough child protection system in the church. From start to finish, this case exemplifies the principles we have looked at so far in the book – in fact it exemplifies them in such a way that you might read this chapter and say to yourself, 'Yeah, right, Rebecca. You're conveniently making this one up to prove your points and conclude the book. You must think I came down in the last shower.'

This story is true. A small amount of poetic licence has been taken on my part in writing about events that happened before I was personally involved – but the licence only relates to periphery trivia that helps the telling of the main facts. Indeed, it is an appalling and wholly preventable testimony to why *Policing Innocence* has been written.

Martin's story

Martin was seven years old, and he was a lonely kind of seven – the dyslexia that hampered his progress at school was exacerbated by being an only child that isolated him at home. Life was generally an uphill climb for one who should have been carefree, but he did have a comforting safety net in the form of older half-siblings inherited from his mother's first marriage, especially David. David was the sort of older brother a younger brother dreams of having.

Martin was sitting at the kitchen table, forcing himself to stare at the reading book he was battling to conquer and worrying about how to complete the worksheet that came with it. His mum was busy at the stove when suddenly the phone rang with the cruellest interruption into their easy silence. He listened with growing fear to her anguished cries.

Dad was dead. He had been involved in a road accident and he was gone.

A couple of years later

Martin shuffled into the church, hoping in vain that no one would see the garish waistcoat he was being forced to wear as usher for his mum's third wedding. The time had passed quickly since Dad had died; the long months were a dismal blur, from the clarity of that phone call through to the stark reality of this celebration.

Miserably handing out service programmes, Martin wasn't celebrating. He had to admit that this new husband was OK, but the guy wasn't Dad and he never would be. Dad had gone . . . though that endless grief wasn't the main cause of Martin's misery today, and neither was the new husband. It was his adult son, Martin's new step-brother, who was the problem.

Jenkins was in his early twenties and owned a house nearby. It was a small, nondescript house, as quiet and ordinary as its owner. Jenkins worked as a carer on an independent basis, which rendered him unaccountable to anyone but the clients who were dependent on him, and only Martin seemed to have noticed that he didn't have many friends.

He had made a beeline for Martin from the day they first met, much to the delight of their wider family.

'Isn't Jenkins a good chap for taking Martin under his wing?' Martin was tired of hearing people say.

'What a super bloke for sacrificing his weekends and having Martin stay with him so the newlyweds can spend time alone.'

'What a true example of brotherly love he is extending, and to one so young and vulnerable as Martin!'

'Poor Martin does find it tough at school, and he still grieves terribly for his father. He needs someone special to look out for him and Jenkins is just the man for the job.'

Jenkins found deep vulnerabilities in Martin – grief, loneliness, insecurity, academic challenges, a mother in need of some space – all of these were open to unquestioned exploitation. Jenkins pushed for trusted time alone with the child and was given as much as he wanted. The adults in the family were as easily groomed as Martin – from the beginning this step-relative was considered a loving brother and never afforded the due caution appropriate to a stranger. He was a professional carer after all – caring for the vulnerable was what he did best . . . wasn't it? No one was suspicious of his overwhelming care towards Martin, not even when that care was specially crafted to be given out of sight from anyone else. With cunning deviousness, Jenkins turned the tables to make it appear that he was generously filling the aching gaps in Martin's life, when the truth was that Martin was being abused to fill the aching gaps in Jenkins's life. No one stopped to ask why this twenty-something was so driven to forego his own social life and offer private hospitality to a child at week-ends. Martin was expected to be grateful for Jenkins's time and attention; complaining about him was not an option. Who would have believed that such a kind man could be a monster behind closed doors, and how could this hurt-ing boy be expected to shoulder responsibility for upset-ting everyone – especially his mum? In the autumn of her life the grieving widow had been given one last chance at happiness, and the fear of being responsible for shattering her contentment secured Martin's silence.

Jenkins sexually abused Martin for a number of years. It was veiled behind a well-groomed pretence that he was helping the boy and allowing the newlyweds some pri-vate time. The systematic abuse took place at Jenkins's house and was never suspected. It was easy for him.

Years later

Sunday lunch, Martin hated it. On a regular basis his family gathered together, never detecting the jagged splinter beneath the surface. Now in his twenties himself, Martin liked seeing Mum surrounded by those she loved. He coped with the cauliflower being boiled to oblivion, and he stomached the way she waited on her husband as though he was royalty who had missed the turn to the palace. But he couldn't abide Jenkins. The man never missed a gathering; he would parade in front of them all, take his plate of soggy veg and smile as though nothing had happened. All those years of abuse, and Jenkins swanned around the family home as though nothing had happened. Martin's wounds were as open and as sore as ever.

Today the cauliflower was so very boiled that a lobster would have felt sorry for it, and Martin laid his fork down beside his plate in culinary defeat. He watched Jenkins shovel his food down regardless, and he remembered the past. It wasn't fair. His own life had been so blighted by Jenkins's destruction – he struggled with the anger and pain, resentment and confusion, restlessness and injustice. The harder he tried to overcome the damage, the more it damaged him and the harder he tried to overcome it. Alone. It was a debilitating cycle he could not break out of. But look at Jenkins – not a care in the world! Shovelling Mum's cooking as though she owed it to him, when he had defiled her son for years.

'Oh Martin,' said Mum. 'Don't be so fussy with your vegetables. There's nothing wrong with that cauliflower. Jenkins, dear, would you like some more?'

Mum's innocent remarks felt loaded; Jenkins was still in control. He had ended the abuse with the same decisive control that he had begun it . . . and then he had walked away. He had walked away without resentment and torment, he had walked away without anger and pain, he had walked away into an honourable marriage with an honourable woman and they had done the honourable thing of producing two grandchildren and going to church. Martin himself had rejected religion, and knew that he was regarded as a contrary young man, obstinate and challenging, a difficult person who was struggling to find his way in the world and who needed to get a grip on life before it passed him by. It wasn't fair. If only they knew what a monumental achievement it was for him to just sit at the same table as Jenkins. If only they knew what monumental obstacles he had faced in his life, and what a monumental challenge it was for him to combat them on a daily basis. In real terms, he had achieved far more in his life than Jenkins would ever aspire to; it was time people knew the truth.

A few weeks later

Martin trudged up the stone steps of the police station for the second time in as many weeks.

Two weeks ago he had climbed them with terrified hope; now he was crushed. It was a new crushing that bore the condemnation of his family as well as the pain of his childhood. He was thankful for David and only David.

A fortnight ago Martin had done the bravest thing of his life: he had sat across a table from a burly police officer and unlocked the chains that shackled his memory. With a resolute courage not many people would have believed he possessed, he had formalized every word of his suffering into a police statement intended to bring Jenkins to justice. With every word he spoke, Martin felt like he was limping into battle against a powerful enemy while wounded, defenceless and alone. The policeman was gentle, and when Martin read the pages at the end, he signed each one to verify it as a true account of his suffering. He had pulled the pin out of the family grenade. He went home and waited for it to detonate, hoping to shelter in their compassion and understanding at last.

It detonated all right. It blew up in his face and hurled the debris at his feet, leaving Jenkins sheltered by their compassion. The family was shell-shocked by the accusation that Jenkins was not the nice, caring, harmless Jenkins they thought they knew, but actually a calculating paedophile who had defiled a young boy in their midst. Mum and new-Dad were torn down the middle; how could Mum's son be the hunted, and Dad's son have been his hunter? How could the couple remain united with such a schism blasted between them? While unchecked horror and unanswered questions orbited the family, Jenkins had one chance to retain control – and he took it. The family emotions were up for grabs – he had to manipulate them before Martin wreaked any more havoc. Jenkins quickly dismissed Martin as a vengeful fantasist and turned the tables again to demean him as the calculating one. With outpourings of apparent regret and shame, Jenkins admitted that their relationship had crossed the line many years ago, but he claimed that the sexual activity had occurred when Martin was far older than he really was, and he grossly reduced the extent of what had physically occurred. Then he gave Martin a final kick in the stomach by assuring everyone that the relationship had been entirely consensual and now Martin was inventing horror stories about child abuse to destroy him. The family had to decide who was lying.

Martin became the troublemaker. Here he was fabricating stories about Jenkins, exaggerating the truth, besmirching the kindness he had been offered as a boy.

'What is Jenkins's wife to make of this?'

'How is Martin's mum to carry on building her marriage?'

'Why has Martin come out with it now? Surely if this story were true he would have said so at the time?'

'Martin has always been difficult and aimless, while Jenkins has always given his life to care for others and serve their needs before his own.'

'Jenkins is happily married and goes to church every week; he's a godly man, no doubt about it.'

The apparently solid, trustworthy Jenkins was pitched against an unsettled, unproven Martin – and Martin lost. The fact that Martin had been a struggling, lonely, bereaved child targeted by a calculating adult predator was buried by the weight of Jenkins's campaign. He ensured that the family judged the two of them in the present day – and in doing so he won a fatal victory over Martin. If Jenkins had been a saucepan he would have been made from Teflon through and through; nothing stuck to him. Martin would have been the old burnt milk pan; longing to shine and please the family, longing to produce something lovely from his life, but tarnished and afflicted by dark burns he could do nothing about.

The family rallied around Jenkins instead of Martin and joined Jenkins in piling pressure on him to retract his police statement. It wasn't fair on Jenkins for Martin to pursue it. David, however, stood firmly with Martin against the familial tide, but his strong support was not enough to withstand the pressure and, full of condemned defeat, Martin returned to the police station and asked for the prosecution to be stopped. He did not withdraw the statement as untrue – he just couldn't cope with carrying the burden of pursuing it. He was a broken man – therefore he was easily bullied into not having the strength to seek justice for what caused that brokenness. The courage he had shown in making the statement in the first place was never credited to him.

Martin left the police station in turmoil, while the family buried the past and tried to forget the horrible virus that had infected them. But David didn't forget.

Three years later

By now, the family had moved on from the horrible stories Martin had told and they had excused Jenkins for supposedly having a consensual relationship with him years ago. It was concluded that they were both relatively young men experimenting with their sexuality, and the sorry details were best left to the archives of their memories. Who was anyone to judge?

For my part, I had recently implemented a child protection system at church. The leadership had asked me to undertake the role because of my police experience working in the field, and my instructions were to prepare as robust a system as possible so that we would be known as a church that passionately protected its children. Every church member who wanted to work with children and young people in any capacity had to complete various paperwork requirements and attend a training evening. No one was allowed to be a children's worker without going through this process. The training evening also included completion of the complex forms necessary for Criminal Record Bureau checks to be submitted. The church was footing the bill for each check, which was no mean sum of money, especially as we were entitled to request enhanced checks that not only queried criminal records but verified if any child-related complaint had ever been made to the police and Social Services, regardless of whether it had resulted in a criminal conviction.

I suspect the membership's general attitude towards these training evenings was similar to the general attitude towards malaria jabs: 'Not pleasant but it's got to be done.' Through reading their slouched body language and stony faces as I spoke, I reckoned they were collectively thinking, 'Sit it out, bear the pain. Humour the old girl and it'll soon be home time. Hey, we might even get a sweetie at the end if we're good.' (Maybe I'm the one who's missing the point, but I still can't fathom why watching television and ironing tomorrow's shirt seems to be a higher priority to some people than learning about how to protect children and *how to protect themselves*.) Thankfully I hadn't expected any encouragement from folk about what I was doing, which was a good job because I didn't get any. Well, no, that's not entirely true. David and Sue Jones did offer to attend the evenings and take on the huge administrative task of examining all the identification required for the Criminal Record forms so that I was free to deliver the training.

This particular evening went by without a hitch and, just as I was leaving, I was approached by one of the elders. He informed me that a member called Jenkins had been present and wanted a copy of my notes to take away because he hadn't heard everything I had said. Wondering why the bloke couldn't have approached me himself, I photocopied the notes and handed them to the elder, thinking nothing of the fact that no one had ever asked this before. Relieved to be finished, I flew home, threw off my shoes and cracked open the bottle of red wine that had been calling me all night. Then the phone rang.

'Hi Rebecca, it's Sue Jones. I have to tell you this, I can't keep it quiet. You said tonight that we must report any concerns we have about protecting children at church. Well, I saw that Jenkins was there tonight. He has completed an application form requesting to work with Sunday school and has done a Criminal Record form – he actually handed it to me himself. Rebecca, I know that Jenkins sexually abused David's younger half-brother Martin for years when Martin was a boy. You won't know him; he doesn't come to church. The truth came out among the family a few years back but nothing official was done against Jenkins. His wife knows and I also need to tell you that he spends his summers working on children's camps, helping youngsters with special needs.'

I questioned Sue closely about what she had said, desperately hoping that each of my questions would disprove the story as firmly as each of her answers was confirming it. The fact that the whole family knew about the allegation, including Jenkins's wife, was compelling, added to the fact that full police and Social Services records were available. Under the umbrella of the children's protection being paramount I could have made direct enquiries with those organizations, or just submitted Jenkins's Criminal Record check to receive the same information. I was left in no doubt that Sue was telling me the truth.

'David and I are so scared now, Rebecca,' she said. 'The family will rally against us for making this phone call. We know that a lot of trouble is ahead for us, but we had to tell you about Jenkins. We couldn't leave him to have access to all those innocent children knowing what we do, but this is going to cost us dearly. It's awful.'

David and Sue were not doing this lightly – they were doing it because they had to. They were doing it because it was true. I didn't bother with a glass – I drank the wine from the bottle.

At 9 a.m. the following morning I sat in the church minister's lounge with the minister and one of the elders. After discussing the content of Sue's call I made it clear that decisive action had to be taken against Jenkins;

such serious allegations required serious actions. While these actions were being processed, I would submit Jenkins's Criminal Record check as a matter of urgency to officially confirm the story, and the minister would speak to Jenkins and seek his account of what had happened. They were both in agreement with this way forward . . . until I spelled the actions out.

- We have to ban him from working with children and young people in the church in any format.
- We have to compile a set of strict boundaries that govern what he can and can't do, and he must abide by them at all times.
- We have to inform relevant Sunday school leaders about him.

This they were in agreement with. Then I continued:

- We have to tell the local Social Services about his own two children.
- We have to tell the camps he helps at, and also the Social Services that cover the locations of the camps.

This they were not so keen on. Through ignorance and not malice they asked, 'Why do we have to do that? Can't we keep this within the church?'

'The protection of children is paramount. All children. What kind of church are we if we put boundaries around our own kids and leave others to run the gauntlet? We have to be thorough. We have to think of every child who features in this mess and put their protection before any other consideration.'

At this point they acquiesced. We agreed that I would create Jenkins's boundaries and the minister would meet with him to explain them and get them signed.

That would leave me free of contact with Jenkins to do the official reporting, and it would leave the minister free of officialdom to be available to Jenkins on a pastoral basis.

When he heard the news Jenkins went into freefall. He had lost control.

A few weeks later

It seemed to me that the 'Jenkins crisis' had been ridden – which was one of the most short-sighted conclusions I have ever reached in my life. The boundaries had been signed and were now in force. The elder assured me that those people within the church who needed to know about Jenkins had been informed, and I had reported the case to the relevant authorities. The minister continued to keep himself out of it, saying that he had to remain neutral in case Jenkins needed him. 'What Jenkins needed'; it became a mantra.

When he learned what had happened, Jenkins stormed round to David and Sue Jones's house and put pressure on them to withdraw what they had told the church. Such pressure had worked before with Martin, so it was worth a try now; somehow he had to regain control of this nightmare. David and Sue were as immovable as they were distressed. They retracted nothing and the nightmare continued – it had many scenes to run before anyone would be finding any peace.

At about this time I had a phone conversation with the minister, during which I couldn't help asking, 'The bit I don't understand is why Jenkins approached Sue Jones with his Criminal Record forms at the training evening in the first place. He knew she was aware of his history and that he could well be exposed if he applied to work with children. Why didn't he walk away when he saw her?'

The minister replied, 'Jenkins never had any intention of working with children. He only attended the evening to get hold of his criminal record and see what was on it. He knew the church has to pay for the check which saved him doing it, and knew the church sends a copy out to his address which was all he wanted.'

Then the minister went on to express sympathy for the desperate worry and fear Jenkins was currently living under. I did not agree with his sentiments.

'Let me get this straight. Jenkins sexually abused Martin for years when he was a young and desperately vulnerable child. When Martin complained to the police, Jenkins pressurized him to withdraw his statement and manipulated the family tide to flow against him. Then recently Jenkins filled in a church Sunday school application and lied outright on it. He lied about not having previous complaints made against him and he lied about his reasons for wanting to work with children, because he didn't want to work with them at all. It was all a crafty scheme to get hold of his criminal record courtesy of our budget and toil by attending the training evening. Which, I must add, he shouldn't have been present at. And, when he was there, he deceptively took possession of my notes which I would never have released to him if I had known he was a paedophile. He must have been frantic about what was on his record to have taken such a risk in front of Sue, the one person who could expose him. And then, as if that wasn't enough deception and cunning, he has pressurized the Joneses to withdraw their report – which constitutes the criminal offence of "witness intimidation" – *and you want me to feel sorry for him?'*

'Actually, Rebecca, I was wondering if you could talk to him and calm his worries a bit.'

'No, I can't. Professionally I have to keep my distance. Beyond my church responsibilities I mustn't get involved in this story, and my loyalty is to the Joneses, not to Jenkins.' When I put the phone down I added, 'I'd rather have a malaria jab.'

Ten months later

As far as John and I were concerned, the Jenkins saga had gone quiet. We knew that David and Sue had told Martin about our comprehensive action at church and that Martin had felt empowered by this news to return to the police and continue with his search for justice. He realized that we had believed him and taken his suffering seriously, and this had revived his own courage to enter into the battle again. This time Jenkins had been arrested, interviewed and formally charged with child sexual abuse offences. He had made partial confessions to the police about what he had subjected Martin to, and was awaiting trial at Crown Court. The impact on the wider family was devastating as David and Sue stood with Martin and everyone else stood with Jenkins – whose carefully manufactured PR bandwagon was unstoppable. To regain control, the bandwagon was constructed of deception upon deception and it advanced unchecked for some time. Until . . .

One Friday morning I received a letter in the post from Jenkins. It outlined a serious accusation of wrongdoing he alleged I had committed against him, and then it forgave me for it at the end. Nice touch. Wondering whether a brass band and cheerleaders were going to jump out of the envelope declaring the wonders of practical jokes I read the letter again, and this time I really absorbed it.

The allegation claimed that I had given Jenkins illegal advice about solicitors and told him not to contact one when he was arrested. This is a serious wrongdoing for any police officer, which invariably leads to the firing squad and then the dole queue. On the basis of my alleged instruction, Jenkins said he had declined legal representation when he was in police custody, and been hoodwinked into making confessions he would not otherwise have made. These confessions had led to the unfortunate charges, and he was expecting the unfortunate charges to lead to imprisonment. Just before the line about forgiving me, Jenkins added that the police, the CPS and his defence team were aware of what he was alleging I had done.

I had never spoken to the bloke in my life. I had never even told him the time.

I knew I could lose my job if I was found guilty of this accusation. And I knew that Jenkins could walk free from justice if his defence used the accusation at court to bring his confessions into question. Because Martin was a difficult young man, he was not perceived as a strong prosecution witness and, without any other evidence, the confessions were the main basis on which Jenkins would be convicted. Discrediting their validity would render a conviction unsafe and acquit him. So, to escape justice, he framed me by alleging that I had framed him.

The arrival of this letter removed the lid from the proverbial can of worms, and we found that it had snakes inside. John and I made many phone calls as we tried to understand what was happening, and were shocked to discover just how busy Jenkins and his wife had been. In the time between being charged and being due at court they had launched a salvage operation at church, designed to absolve him and win over people's hearts – and they had succeeded. This is what we learned.

- Martin had been painted in the same bad light as when Jenkins had maligned him to his family. The fact that he was a difficult young man in the present day (who could have had Jenkins for breakfast if he'd chosen to take such revenge) was cruelly used to distract people from the fact that he had been such a fragile child years ago. I repeatedly protested about this vicious distortion with various people: 'Martin is difficult now because Jenkins damaged him so badly – and how the poor guy presents now is completely irrelevant anyway.' I was desperately trying to redress the balance and rescue the truth, but I never managed to. The Jenkinses had rammed their version into people's thinking with such deafening precision that the truth could not be heard. Martin became the aggressor – Jenkins his victim.

- The accusation about me was passed around the church and the story largely accepted. 'Rebecca Andrews has misbehaved and Jenkins is in deep trouble because of her lack of integrity.' Some people began avoiding John and me on a Sunday morning, clearly conveying their displeasure and not wanting to be seen with such unsavoury characters as two allegedly bent police officers. We were perceived as the toughie coppers and Jenkins the poor old soul we had framed. We became the aggressors – Jenkins our victim.

- From this victimized standpoint, Jenkins requested a number of character witnesses from people within the church to present to the court. He approached highly qualified individuals with great standing in the community and, despite these people being enviously clever and full of professional child protection training, they were drawn into Jenkins's web of deceit and supported him. Can you imagine how powerful such a team of character witnesses were for him before the judge – especially when Martin was unable to muster the same?

- The success of any campaign rests on how far to the top it can reach – and this effort basked on high. The church leadership was firmly in Jenkins's camp and deftly removed themselves from the fact that they had agreed to the original church actions against him. The fallout was going very sour, and it was easier to make it the Andrews's fault. The leadership adopted Jenkins's account, including the accusation against me, and aligned themselves with this apparently needy man. Indeed, they were the ones who encouraged him to write to me and offer forgiveness. Jenkins's many deceptions – which I often reiterated – were excused as confusions, misunderstandings, and the panicked actions of a terrified man who deserved pity. The fact that he was a calculating paedophile in complete control of them all was not acknowledged. That wasn't for the want of trying on my part, though! I persisted in trying to take the wool away from their eyes, but I think the more I harped on, the less they believed me . . . and the more they thought I was maligning Jenkins to escape my own supposed wrongdoings.

Here lies the brilliance of Jenkins's campaign. Let me try and describe him to you. He is a very ordinary man to look at and seems extremely quiet to the point of being withdrawn. He presents as being of lower-than-average intelligence and is not a person of flair or charisma; my prevailing image of him is that he shuffles about as though he is trying to be invisible. Why am I telling you this? The simple man I have just described deceived countless highly intelligent people into believing his unbelievable version of events. I frankly think that was rather brilliant of him. He knew they saw him as some kind of downtrodden figure, so he manipulated this weakness into becoming his strength and presented himself as so very downtrodden he could have been mistaken for the pavement. He inspired only pity and never suspicion. The fact that he had held a powerful grip over a grieving boy was impossible for them to comprehend when they could see nothing powerful about him. The fact that he was driving a clever falsehood against me was impossible for them to comprehend when they could see nothing clever about him.

Isn't misperception one of the great iniquities of paedophilia? Some adults judge offenders from their adult standpoint and project that judgement on to the child; if they think the offender is pathetic they dismiss the reality that to the child he is powerful. I beg you never to fall into this trap. It is the child we are protecting, and it is their knowledge and perception that counts. If your little one is scared of the dark, do you dismiss that terror because it holds no fear for you? Their perception is the true reality, and a child in fear of a monstrous sex offender means the man is monstrous – whether or not the adult perceives him to be a harmless idiot.

Everyone Jenkins targeted among the congregation was made to feel sorry for him and with overwhelming Christian compassion they danced to his tune. He made them feel that *he* was the one in need of protection; true reality was lost and never recovered. Did you note the word 'targeted'? He didn't print what was happening in the church news sheet for all to see; he very carefully selected who he used.

And as for me framing him – it wouldn't have made any sense. Leaving issues of my faith and integrity aside, breaking the rules to frame him would have risked incurring the loss of my career, my income, my pension and my reputation. For me to have taken a gamble with such high stakes would have needed Jenkins to have been massively important in my life. He simply wasn't.

The next day

Jenkins made a mistake. He got his timing wrong. He sent my letter the day before his trial and it arrived at our house quickly. This tipped me off about how he planned to use his accusation against me to escape justice and it gave me time to take the necessary action. A flurry of phone calls and reports were completed and I was ready to defend myself at his trial. I will always believe this was the work of God. I have thanked him over and over again for giving me this chance to clear my name and, at the eleventh hour, Jenkins's defence declined to use the accusation in court and, with the confessions, upheld he was found guilty. For his many years of child sexual abuse he went to prison for twelve months – due to be released after six of them if he behaved himself.

At court, David sat with Martin on one side of the public gallery and no one else sat with them. On the other side of the gallery were a large number of church members – including leadership – who had gathered to support Jenkins. This impressed the judge (I know because he said so) and it biased the judgement he delivered in Jenkins's favour. Don't forget these weren't just 'people', these were 'church people'; rightly or wrongly there's an assumption of virtue that comes with that. Churches are so up for misuse in this area – even ones with comprehensive child protection systems who claim to know what they're doing. I wonder what the judge concluded from the fact that the seats around Martin were empty.

Jenkins's careful grooming of the church family paid him dividends. This tactic, coupled with the next tactic both worked a treat; you see, his next tactic was to plead guilty to 60 per cent of what had happened and assert

that it was 100 per cent. This is commonplace for paedophiles who make confessions. The general consensus
is that the 60 must be 100 because it isn't a denial, and no
one looks any further because the 60 secures a conviction, thus maintaining budgets and targets. For Martin,
though, it was another wielding of the axe. It cut him
deeply when the judge commended Jenkins as noble
and good for telling the truth, when Martin knew it was
merely a partial truth for which he was being given full
credit. Partial truths should receive partial credit. And
then the axe struck again when the twelve-month sentence was delivered – the abuse had lasted for years and
its destruction looked set to damage for a lifetime, but
Jenkins was being imprisoned for a dim shadow of the
sentence he had inflicted on Martin.

Martin and David left court as shattered men that day,
but the axe hadn't finished its work. They arrived home
to discover that some family members had received letters of apology from Jenkins – but not Martin. The judge
had specifically credited Jenkins for seeking absolution
for his crimes, and yet the one human being Jenkins
needed to seek absolution from had been omitted from
his list. As far as I am aware, he has still not apologized
to Martin and, even now, he is still upheld for having
done it. Apologizing to other people *except* Martin was
cruel, deliberate and cowardly – it would have been
more palatable if he hadn't said sorry to anyone.
Leading others into believing that he *had* apologized to
him was another deception that fuelled the bandwagon's advance.

So I believe Jenkins took advantage of Martin to the
bitter end, mainly because he groomed people into
thinking that he was not capable of doing so. I have to
say, I was and still am deeply sorry about the terrible
wrong Jenkins inflicted on Martin, and am deeply

ashamed of the disrespect shown to him by the justice system and others.

Three months later

John and I were informed that Jenkins was behaving very well in prison and holding up under the strain. The leadership knew this because they were travelling the long distance to prison to visit him every week. He became the church's most visited member while he was behind bars – and I would have no problem with that if it wasn't for the fact that the Joneses didn't receive so much as a phone call. John and I weren't too worried about whether Jenkins was being good or ghastly in prison; our concern was about the turmoil Martin and the Joneses were in. To this day I have never met or spoken with Martin, but David and Sue told us how much he was struggling with the rejection of his family and the failure of the legal system – justice had not felt like justice to him. David and Sue were in no better place themselves. They too encountered a sharp backlash from their family for being the catalyst to Jenkins's plight (*his what?*), and, when they turned to their church family for support, they were bitterly disappointed. To be fair, many people were unaware of the case and therefore had no idea that the Joneses *needed* support, but those that did know chose to care for Jenkins. A 'them-and-us' developed in the church where it seemed people felt unable to look out for 'both sides': either they supported Jenkins or they supported us and the Joneses, but not both. Jenkins made sure of that by attributing an element of culpability to us for his imprisonment: Martin had told lies about him, the Joneses had ratted on him, and the Andrewses had framed him. Yes, amazingly lots of bright people accepted it was partly our collective responsibility that Jenkins was in the clink. You've got to admit there are not many spin doctors whirling round Westminster who can wangle a coup like that! Such distortion takes some doing. It doesn't take intellect, it takes cunning – there's a very big difference between the two.

John and I were bound by the confidentiality of our role as child protection co-ordinators throughout the Jenkins saga – but the Joneses were not. At any time they could have blown the whistle to the wider membership to seek revenge or elicit support. They could have split the church into pieces if they had hit back, but they retained a courageous and dignified silence that honoured Christ; they behaved with fantastic composure and honour throughout those awful months.

Part of the leadership's delight at Jenkins's good behaviour in prison was that he was testifying about his Christian faith to other prisoners and telling them how well the church had supported him. They were thrilled by his bold witness – and I agree that such testimony is always lovely – but with sex offenders you must never let your guard down.

I pointed out the following to the leaders.

'That's great on one level but, because he is segregated with other paedophiles, that means the only type of prisoners he will be talking to is fellow paedophiles. By the nature of their crimes they are reviled people in the community, and Jenkins reporting that our congregation is a good place for sex offenders will be music to their lonely ears. The church is now in danger of being inundated by hungry paedophiles. He is putting our children at great risk.'

Have you heard of a lead balloon? My response went down faster.

'Rebecca, that's so sad. You have become dreadfully cynical and neurotic.'

Four months later

I had to regretfully stand down from leading the church child protection system. Much as I loved the role, John and I agreed that professionally I could not risk another serious accusation being levelled against me; I had to remove myself from the line of fire. Jenkins had left me no choice; I had to safeguard my own family and employment. It saddened me, though, and my inevitable resignation was another coup for Jenkins. At a time when the church was at its greatest risk of being flooded by a tidal wave of paedophiles, the role of child protection co-ordinator lost its most qualified (and most vocal) advocate. What a sinister weakening of the long-term protection offered to the church children and what a grubby legacy for Jenkins to have to bear. The fallout seemed endless, especially as the case of Mr I from Chapter 4 was just beginning.

Jenkins had been out of prison for a month by now and was back at church. This was not an easy time for anyone involved, especially when he introduced a new deception to his bandwagon by claiming that he had been maltreated by the police when he was first arrest-ed. This too was believed by some, and cultivated additional sympathy for him. I could imagine his supporters patting him on the back and exclaiming: 'Gosh Jenkins, if John and Rebecca Andrews are anything to go by, you did well to get out of the nick alive, old boy.' (Oh dear, am I getting just a bit too sensitive now?)

When a prisoner is in police custody their detention is video and audio recorded. *Jenkins was not maltreated.* And I'm sure he would have mentioned it at his trial if he was.

A few weeks after his early release, Jenkins arrived at church with a new friend. The Joneses spotted the friend before we did and when Sue pointed him out to me, I groaned.

'The bloke's got to be from prison,' I whispered to John during the notices, 'which means he's got to be a paedophile.'

We quickly decided that although I had stood down from child protection responsibility, the church youngsters were too precious a treasure to abandon, and the identity of the visitor had to be ascertained. A fleeting worry about my reputation for being 'cynical and neurotic' was swiped away with the realization that the 'church youngsters' included our children too. We had to know if the man was a convicted paedophile. John and I raised our concern with the leadership after the service, and they did not agree that the man should be checked out. We tried to reason that protecting the kids from a possible predator overrode every other factor; their innocent right to be safe at church had to be the priority. They weren't having it.

We couldn't leave it there. The consequences of the danger were more awful than our fear of false accusation or our fragile position at church. We had a right in law to identify the man because protecting the children was paramount, and if he was fresh out of prison he would be accountable to the Sex Offenders Register regarding his contact with children. We rang the leadership and warned them that if they didn't identify him and ensure that he was safe, we would call the authorities into the church to do it for them. Under this threat the leadership did approach Jenkins, who eventually admitted that his friend was a paedophile from prison. We didn't glean any pleasure from hearing that, or from reminding the minister that if Jenkins was befriending paedophiles then his own children were at the greatest risk of all. We also didn't glean any pleasure from hearing that the offender refused to return to church upon being identified. What did he need secrecy for?

There are many more things I could say here, but suffice to say that while working hard to 'save' Jenkins, our church 'lost' Martin and exposed all our children to danger. Our first priority must always be to protect children.

After the dust from Jenkins's release had settled, John approached Jenkins's wife and asked if we could all meet together to seek some resolution. He made it clear that it was an open long-term invitation, and suggested that we met at a neutral venue with a third party present, both of which we were happy for Jenkins and his wife to decide. They refused, and resolution has never been sought. I have still never spoken to the bloke.

Another three years later

That is the concise version of the Jenkins saga; the full version would extend this book to a trilogy. The last I heard of Martin was that he was working in the building trade and he and his fiancée had just become proud parents. The Joneses continue to attend the church, having leaned on a tight circle of friends who were brought into the picture to provide the support they needed. Their faith in God sustained them, and they made that imperative distinction between people being the fallible ones and God always remaining perfect. He is never to blame when others mess up. We have just left the church due to relocating for work. Again, our Christian faith deepened in the crisis as God was the unfailing Rock that we clung to in the storm. We also walked that painful but powerful road which is the only constructive way forward when you have been hurt – forgiveness. *Forgiveness* is not for wimps. It takes a lot of guts because it means treading out tough steps that go against the current of everything else you're feeling. There is a magnificent difference between forgiveness and justice. The former is ours to undertake with God's help, and the latter is his to undertake without our help. To offer forgiveness does not mean that justice has been done – it means that you are released from the equation, and it's such a blessed release. To the best of my knowledge, Jenkins continues to attend the church and remains employed as a professional carer.

This chapter has not been written to take a swipe at churchgoers – quite the opposite. John and I love 'church' and the principle of it as a group of people who come together to grow in their faith and serve their communities. This chapter has been written to *help* churches and encourage people to be careful about how they conduct themselves so that we can be proud of our congregations as safe and sensible places.

Listen! We were an ordinary congregation serving an ordinary community. These problems are not rare; they are sickeningly commonplace, and they thrive on congregations denying they exist. The biggest gift a fellowship could hand to any abusers in their midst is to presume that they couldn't possibly be there: 'Not in our church.'

It has to be said: apart from Jenkins's crimes, the biggest failing of this whole story is the willingness of swathes of people to fall for his many deceptions. His persona of being somewhat pathetic and needy masked an unbridled craftiness that successfully manufactured his weakness into his strength. Jenkins was a wolf disguised in sheep's clothing, which is why people only ever wanted to graze with him and not apply the common sense that would have exposed him. And what is it that Jesus says when we are sheep living among wolves? In the Gospel of Matthew (10:16) Jesus instructs us to have the innocence of doves and the shrewdness of snakes. He couldn't have put it more clearly. He himself knew the dangers of deception we would face and commands us to be wise and shrewd, *not* bumble along as well-meaning old fools.

I beg you to question and question sex offenders in your midst. Do not be distracted and fooled by blanket compassion; Jesus wasn't. He made it clear that compassion has its rightful place – as half of a whole that is balanced out with wisdom. If an offender says he has had his children removed, or has had allegations made against him, or he has been to prison for sex crimes and it was all a miscarriage of justice – do yourself a favour and question his claim long and hard. The strongest sex offence cases can fail at court because this area of crime is notoriously incompatible with court processes; if it is hard enough to rightly convict the guilty, I assure you, it is far harder still to wrongly convict the innocent. If someone has been reported at all, then formally charged by the police, then the case approved for trial by the CPS, and the defendant found guilty by a jury, and then sent to prison and not even given a community order – then the chances are that he did it. The likelihood of him being innocent is so microscopic it makes an amoeba appear overweight.

Please don't allow a Jenkins case to occur in your church or your workplace or your home. Apply the biblical principles of compassion and shrewdness in equal measure – always measuring even them by the ultimate principle of the protection of children being paramount. It is Christ-like to do so.

You couldn't make it up

All I have to say here is: 'I wish I was making it up.' Tragic, isn't it?

Postscript:

There Must Be an Answer Somewhere

So what is The Answer? How do we find a way to deal with paedophiles effectively that promotes child safety and then considers offenders' needs too? We sure haven't found it yet. The justice system doesn't seem to know what to do about paedophiles, mainly because it's got its priorities wrong. We need to find The Answer primarily from the point of view of protecting children; it is from their perspective we must approach what to do about the abusers – and that's where the system has lost its way in recent years. I think it's controlled by offenders' needs and its own limitations, ahead of promoting child safety, which is comprehensively failing children.

Sarah's Law

In June 2007, the Home Secretary announced that the decision had been taken not to introduce 'Sarah's Law' in this country – the British version of the American 'Megan's Law' – under which communities are informed about specific paedophiles living in their midst. The law has an element of controversy about it with valid points made on either side of the argument. Let's take a simplified look at them and you can make up your own mind about its merits.

The official argument cited against the implementation of 'Sarah's Law' is mainly based on concerns about vigilantism. The government is worried that identifying offenders would put them at risk of attack, and it also cites cases where unknown offenders have struck; thus claiming that so many unknown predators are out there it wouldn't make much difference to children's safety just to highlight the known ones. The other main argument is the possibility that offenders would be driven 'underground' if identified.

All of these arguments have merit, but they have to be weighed on those vital scales of the children's protection being paramount to really gauge their strength.

The first argument about vigilantism seeks to protect offenders before it seeks to protect children – for that reason it is found wanting on the scales. The second argument fairly states that there are unknown offenders out there ready to strike at any time – the implementation of 'Sarah's Law' would not change that either way – but it would help us guard against the ones we *do* know about, which has to be better than nothing. That argument is found wanting on the scales too. The third argument about offenders disappearing 'underground' is trickier. I do not have statistics for how prevalent a problem this is in America, but our current English system already allows for a measure of information release to certain people and I am not aware of a major 'underground' fall-out as a result. Certainly the disappearance of identified offenders would be a possibility and this is the only argument against 'Sarah's Law' that balances the scales because it does have the potential to compromise the protection of children. I'm confident, though, that this isn't the reason the government has turned the law down. I wonder if it fears the possibility of widespread lawsuits under the Human Rights Act as a result of 'Sarah's Law'? Maybe acts of vigilantism would enable offenders to sue the government for implementing legislation that does not apparently enshrine their human right to live in privacy and safety. If such a lawsuit ever happened, we would need to counter it with victims asking about how their right to privacy and safety is enshrined through the early release of countless sex offenders into communities that do not know who they are and have scant official resources to monitor them.

Essentially I support 'Sarah's Law'. Most other dangers around my children are illuminated for them to see: matches have warnings on the boxes, pylons have fences round them, motorways disallow pedestrians, kettles have safety mechanisms and protective flexes, playgrounds have soft surfaces to cushion their fall. But paedophiles are anonymous and invisible – yet they are arguably as dangerous as danger gets. Concerns about vigilantism feature way down my list of priorities and, as we have seen, paedophiles operate best in secretive conditions. It enables them to maintain control and be supremely devious. If we have a chance to smash some of that secrecy we need overwhelming reasons *not* to take it. It does not rest easy with me that this country has resisted 'Sarah's Law' in fear that paedophiles will be hurt by vigilantes, thus continuing to furnish paedophiles with the secrecy they need to hurt children. However, I do have two reservations.

1. 'Sarah's Law' wouldn't make paedophiles go away or diminish their drive to abuse. They are obsessed and committed people, and they would find a way

around the hazards identification would present to them.

2. I fear it has the potential to lull parents into a false sense of security. It could defeat its very object if parents placed overdue reassurance in it and lowered their protective guard: 'I haven't been notified about any paedophiles living in my street, therefore there are no paedophiles living in my street.' Whether we know about them or not, there are paedophiles living all over the place. The one silver lining to the cloud of not being informed is that we have to remain extremely vigilant about our children's safety because of the very fact that we don't know.

And, folks, do you really trust the system to implement 'Sarah's Law' effectively? Do you think officials would design a slick enough procedure to cope with constantly providing millions of households with updates about thousands of paedophiles changing address on a regular basis? I think efficiency would be buried under backlogs and appeals and mistakes as the administration of the law degenerated into a clerical fiasco. No disrespect to 'Sarah's Law', but I can't think of a government department with the money and competence to make it work.

I want to take a quick look at the three main options we currently have for dealing with dangerous child sex offenders, all of which are intended to be viable alternatives to prison. Don't forget that 'dealing with' is supposed to cover all the angles: punishment, deterrent, justice, rehabilitation and, somewhere along the line, child protection.

1. Therapy

Rehabilitation programmes are available across the country for convicted paedophiles. They are delivered by forensic psychologists in conjunction with other organizations like the Probation Service. The programmes are voluntary and rely on the offenders' co-operation to be successful, they usually last for about nine months and are undertaken both inside prison and beyond it. The two primary goals of rehabilitation are to 1) tear down the brick wall that the offender has built in their mind to facilitate child sexual abuse and 2) restructure it into a healthy and lawful way of thinking. It's a mammoth undertaking. I would like to say here that the few psychologists I have met retain a commendable sense of humour amid the nature of their work – I salute you!

- Rehabilitation is tough. It requires the complete overhauling of an individual's old mindset into a radical new way of operating. It is a tough enough achievement for those who do want to co-operate and, as we saw in Chapter 3, an estimated 90 per cent of offenders do not want to co-operate.
- Rehabilitation is voluntary with no penalty incurred for refusing it. That means the paedophiles are dictating the odds to the system about whether they do or do not receive help. Imagine what they say when they are asked to participate: 'Hmm, that's a hard decision, officer. Shall I or shall I not rehabilitate? Tough question; I'd rather you asked me one on sport. To be honest, right now I just feel like having a beer, so can we talk about this therapy stuff another time? It makes no difference to me, anyway; you've still got to let me out.' The balance of power needs redressing if rehabilitation is to be given a more significant role.
- Don't forget that if rehabilitation is given a more significant role under the present set-up, offenders would effectively be choosing whether they submit to

the justice system or not. What other criminals are given such a choice? And these are among the most devastating criminals we have. It is outrageous that offenders can call the shots like this; the system needs to acquire itself a backbone – fast.

- There are not enough professionals equipped to deliver the therapy at this time. There are certainly not enough available to rely on it as a principal method of dealing with offenders – that would require a huge extending of the already inadequate provision.
- If an offender is released early or never sent to prison on the basis that he will co-operate with rehabilitation, he is untreated at the beginning of the process and only partially treated for most of its duration. It takes months for therapy to take effect – and throughout those months, *before the therapy has worked*, he is untethered, barely monitored, and surrounded by the circumstances that lured him into committing his offences. He remains a free and highly tempted danger.
- I think the justice system should punish, deter, prevent and protect as well as rehabilitate. Therapy does not tick all these boxes and shouldn't be expected to.

I think that rehabilitation has a part to play in dealing with paedophiles, but it should not be relied upon to take the leading role.

2. Drugs

The government is placing a lot of importance in developing a programme of drug therapy to treat offenders. Volunteers would sign up for a course of chemical treatment designed to suppress libido and prevent offending.

- The drug option relies on volunteers. Ninety per cent of sex offenders are refusing to participate in therapy – which is of far less personal cost than the drugs option – so the likelihood of masses of them signing up to have their sexual libido chemically suppressed is slim indeed.
- Those that do volunteer will need to persevere with the treatment; my guess is that out of the very few who would be willing to start, a substantial amount would drop out of the programme before the end. They would be surrounded by all kinds of powerful temptation constantly triggering their sexual attraction to children, and the strength of willpower they would need to continue with the programme is a rare phenomenon.
- The government has not mentioned what incentive there would be for offenders to agree to drug treatment. Chemically suppressing libido is a serious step to take and I struggle to believe that offenders will not be offered something in return for volunteering, especially as the government is going to want to attract high numbers to show that the programme is working. I dread to think what incentives would be considered – lighter sentencing, less restrictions on where they work, less information released?
- Drugs may suppress the physical compulsion to act sexually, but they do not change the workings of a paedophile's mind – and that is the source of his sexual attraction to children. Could drugs increase Internet offending as an alternative for men whose physical response is suppressed but their mind is still ticking?

I think that drugs have a part to play in dealing with paedophiles, but they should not be relied upon to take the leading role.

Accountability

I have never heard 'accountability' mentioned when these treatments are discussed. Surely they are only truly viable if they are underpinned by the accountability of the professionals delivering them. Who will determine that crucial point in an offender's progress when he is deemed to have recovered? Someone will need to make the decision that sufficient therapy and/or chemicals have been input and he is no longer a threat requiring the system's attention. Will that person be held accountable for their decision? If not, why not? Personally I think that professionals should be held accountable when they pronounce an offender 'safe' who then goes on to commit unspeakable things and clearly isn't safe enough to keep a guinea pig let alone walk the streets of freedom. I think our current judges and specialists would make more careful decisions by a completely different set of criteria if they were held to account for their judgements. If we restored some accountability, we'd restore some common sense.

Funding

And the money? A finite budget will be allocated to these treatments – so a finite amount of treatment will be available, putting pressure on the staff to prioritize offenders and advance them through the programmes as quickly as possible. Paedophiles commit highly personalized crimes according to highly personalized motivations – so it follows that they need highly personalized treatment. The costs and labour required to deliver such individual help on a vast scale would be prohibitive, and could dilute treatment programmes into becoming generalized conveyor belts that process lots of offenders, but barely transform any of them.

3. Information release

'Sarah's Law' would have enabled communities to know the identity of convicted paedophiles living in their area. Currently, we have a very limited version of that which allows for some release of details to critical people most directly affected by a known offender: employers, family members, voluntary groups, religious organizations, etc. This allowance is certainly a start and it helps – as we saw when our church was entitled to identify the friend that Jenkins brought along from prison. The main failing of our current system is a chronic lack of staff to manage it expeditiously. The volume of offenders compared to the volume of staff is pitiful; it's like using nail scissors to cut the lawn. Vast amounts get missed out. The shortage of personnel leads to frequent information breakdowns, a burdensome amount of tasks and paperwork, inevitable mistakes, widespread use of false identities by offenders that no one has the time to investigate, and thousands of offenders simply falling off the authorities' radar altogether. Any increase in the release of information to protect children would be fantastic, but the personnel to manage the release would be better.

I think that information release has a part to play in dealing with paedophiles, but it should not be relied upon to take the leading role.

Conclusion

We cannot rely on these three methods to keep children safe. Why? They all rely on us trusting offenders in some measure. Paedophiles are inherently devious people; we cannot design a justice system that relies on trusting them. It is doomed.

Paedophiles are the ultimate deceivers. Trusting them to agree to therapy and drugs programmes in the first place, then trusting them to co-operate and not just sit the courses out to win freedom is not the way to fight a successful war. Make no bones about it, we are at war with paedophiles. They are on one side, tactically encroaching on our children's innocence and we are the only people on the other side who can vanquish this foe. Toothless, side-stepping policies are not the way to fight the war: we've got to be cleverer, more determined, and more ruthless than they are.

Does our system strike you as being as fiercely driven to protect children as paedophiles are fiercely driven to abuse them? No, it doesn't strike me like that either! We can't deal with paedophiles in a way that allows them any room for manoeuvre, and leaning too heavily on programmes that can be refused or duped allows offenders more space to manoeuvre than I need to park my car . . . and that's a lot of space. Rehabilitation and drugs treatment do sometimes work, but they are not a quantifiable science and they hold no guarantees. It is arguable that if offenders had the awesome willpower required to make these treatments effective long-term, they would not have succumbed to their offences in the first place. On their own, rehabilitation and drugs programmes are not a sufficient antidote to the epidemic problem of child sexual abuse ravaging our country.

And where is the punishment for the crime? Paedophiles do terrible things to children with devastating consequences that last for a lifetime. It is right that they are punished for this – rehabilitation and drugs programmes do not penalize. They seek to address the cause of the crime and prevent further offences but they do not punish the horror that has already been inflicted.

Prison

What do I think should happen? I think sex offenders should go to prison. I think they should go to prison for a long time. In fact, I think they should go to prison for exactly the amount of time the lawbooks stipulate. The inept sentences you read about in the newspapers are not what the law books say – they are what the policies and guidelines say. The actual lawbooks say that rapists should go to prison for life – not ten years reduced to five for good behaviour. They say that offenders who watch indecent images of children should go to prison for months and years, not receive police cautions. It's all there – the legislative powers we need to lock pae-dophiles far away from vulnerable children. For some reason, the legal profession has just lost the will to use it. The law needs to flex its muscles to protect children, not bend at the knee to cater for offenders.

Appropriate and rigorous imprisonment that makes no apology for its boldness guarantees that child preda-tors are off the streets. *That* allows for therapy and drugs to be administered without pressure and without risk over a sensible period of time. Full monitoring can be conducted to clarify how genuinely an offender has sought to rehabilitate long before he is released, and a fair measure of punishment and deterrent is included in the process. Rehabilitation and drugs programmes do not suit everyone; offenders can attend therapy in name alone but resist true change, and voluntary chemical treatment is, at best, sporadic in its reliability. Imprisonment is universal – it cannot be deceived, resisted, lied about, or given up on.

Most importantly, children are protected and respected by the law when paedophiles are incarcerated for meaningful lengths of time. Imprisonment ticks all the boxes. (All the sensible ones anyway.) The money could be made available through the millions saved when offenders are not free to offend: their offences cost the taxpayer an obscene amount of money across the whole spectrum of public services. Has the contradiction ever struck you? Politicians routinely complain that they cannot afford to lock paedophiles up, but from the same purse they are willing to pay for alternative treatments that cost them just as much and cost children their safety – even, sometimes, their lives. I think the financial argument against imprisonment is a red herring – if this country has the money to treat offenders, it has the money to lock them up. I don't know the exact figures, but I reckon it could actually be cheaper to imprison paedophiles than foot the many bills for treatment: organizing the programmes, the training, the venues, the drugs, the monitoring, the meetings, the consultations, the information releases, the lawsuits, the staffing, the policing, and the multi-faceted clear-up operations incurred by re-offending. And finally: The advantage of imprisonment is that it offers a supreme level of protection to children that the treatments cannot match. That's priceless. *Imprisonment can be relied upon to take the leading role.*

Full and proper prison sentences are not revolutionary – they are what the law has said for years but the courts have stopped applying it. Paedophiles show no leniency to children – the law must not show leniency to them. Until we devise something even more reliable, we must send paedophiles to prison to uphold the protection of children as paramount. And while they're in there, let's be sensible and not closet them together – that doesn't punish or rehabilitate them, it facilitates future offences. Segregation is the only logical way of assisting rehabilitation – otherwise offenders return from an hour's daily therapy to twenty-three hours of fantasizing in a cell with like-minded individuals. That doesn't give rehabilitation much chance of tearing down the old mental walls and building up new ones.

Imprisonment is not a perfect solution, I accept, but it has to be better than the legal merry-go-round we have now.

The fact is, until a watertight environment is created in our society through stringent sentencing, compulsory therapy programmes, penalties for those who do not co-operate and no tolerance of re-offending, childcarers must maintain a fortress of protection around their children. The system places great value in the rights of offenders to be looked after – childcarers are the only ones who are going to place great value in the rights of their children to be looked after. When sex offenders are released into the community the authorities do not have a safety net to catch and contain them; they are pretty much as free as you and me. So we must create the safety net around children in our care.

There are those who say that locking offenders up in prison doesn't work. As far as I can see, the 'locking them up' bit works fine – it's the 'letting them go' bit that wreaks havoc on society.

The grace of God

That's the human level – but this is God's world and his sovereignty is the final justice for us all. Jesus' love for humankind has no walls or ceilings; his forgiveness and welcome is vast enough for us all without prejudice or condition. When he died and rose again he won the ultimate victory over all sin and all death which means that nothing is bigger or greater than he is. That includes child sexual abuse. Jesus loves paedophiles. He doesn't love what they do – *he abhors it* – but he loves the individuals and is fully committed to them living in restored and honest relationship with him. Jesus wants to walk through life with paedophiles as much as he wants to walk through life with police officers.

I believe that the grace of Jesus is an open invitation to come to him just as we are without needing to worry about whether we're good enough. None of us are. There's nothing any of us do that he struggles to cope with, nothing he hasn't seen and heard before. When we accept his invitation to submit our lives to his power, it is the most fantastic and imperative decision we can make. It is a decision of privilege and of responsibility. The privilege comes from the fact that God Almighty, the Maker of heaven and earth, deigns to love us humans and wants to commune with us. Here I am, a bit of dust on this planet for a few fleeting years, and God wants to know me. Now that's what I call a privilege. The responsibility that comes with it is a commitment to try to live according to God's ways and thoughts for the rest of my days. Of course I fail as much as I manage it, but I never stop trying.

The grace of Jesus can forgive and restore paedophiles. I believe only Christ has the real power and means to triumph over the inner disturbance that the best human rehabilitative efforts don't quite manage to reach. Paedophilia is innate, it's defined in someone's mind and being. But as mysteriously as it begins, it can mysteriously end – and it's God's mystery. If there was a human remedy – a true, long-lasting, trustworthy remedy – I think we would have located it by now. The only true remedy to paedophilia is the power of Jesus. The Bible says that he is the way, the truth and the life (see John's Gospel, 14:6). The Bible is God's Word and, as such, it cannot lie. Co-operating with Christ is the way that paedophiles can rediscover the truth and finally live *life* as it should be lived.

It's that word 'co-operating' again. It may be enough to satisfy human requirements but it isn't enough to satisfy God. His call is not for us to merely co-operate with him but to utterly renounce our old ways of living and adopt his character from the very depths of who we are. I have been a committed Christian for many years and the God I have learned about does not want just my co-operation, he wants all of me: my all-out submission and devotion, my all-out acceptance of his authority, my all-out relinquishment to his standards. Co-operation is not enough. I co-operate with the bear-like security girl at the airport who thinks that patting my bra strap ensures I am safe to fly on a plane. I co-operate with the shop assistant who closes the checkout just as I begin unloading my shopping after a thirty-minute wait and my daughter announces, 'I need the toilet.' But I relinquish my life to God. As far as the east is from the west is the difference between the two. How much easier things would be if I could dilute the bits of my faith that are uncomfortable with a shallow co-operation that keeps me in control, pays lip-service to God and cons everyone else, only to milk the bits I do like for my own purposes. No, that's not true Christianity, that's not why Jesus was crucified and it sure isn't why God the Father raised him from the dead.

A paedophile who is serious about his faith has to make the same decision of renunciation and live by it unconditionally. He must submit and devote himself to God which means everything must change, from the inner workings of his mind to the compulsive deceptions of his behaviour. It takes time, it takes sacrifice, it takes transparency. It takes a capitulation to the laws of the land without trying to circumvent them on the back of faith in Christ. It takes an acceptance that he is treated differently around children until the day he dies – he cannot be trusted as fully given over to God if he doesn't comply with sensible boundaries in operation around him. A truly redeemed sex offender would actually *want* to be respected in this way; he would welcome the assistance towards recovery and self-protection and not seek to go anywhere near a child for fear of temptation or false accusation. He would not expect people to pretend that he does not have the history behind him that he has; all of our histories shape our futures and paedophiles are no different. Just as a reformed alcoholic steers clear of the pub for the rest of their days, a reformed paedophile should steer clear of children. If he is truly living in the grace of God he will be gracious towards those who assist him to live carefully and appropriately.

Let me make this analogy: if a well-known thief and gangster became a Christian and joined a church, it would not be wise or appropriate to make him treasurer, responsible for the accounts. But the true measure of his submission to Christ would have been that *he wouldn't want to do it*. He'd join the congregation with a commitment to honesty and rehabilitation that went like this: 'I was a thief, a gangster. God has mercifully redeemed me. I want you to fully know my past so that you can support me in deepening my present transformation and growing up into the future God has for me. I want nothing to do with money or peace-making at church because they are not my strengths. They hold too much temptation for me and I do not want to be vulnerable to misunderstanding or false accusation. If I ever find that I am regressing in my walk with Christ I will quickly tell you so that you can help me cope – you'll need to miss me out when the offering plate goes by. Absolutely nothing must come my way that could compromise or distract me, so I don't even want to go near the "Lost Property" store . . . all those mislaid keys and purses . . . it would be terrible.'

God's grace is for paedophiles. It is for them to embrace, respect and never misuse. It is for them to recover, redeem and never masquerade behind. It is for them to be honest and open and *never* demean as a bypass around personal responsibility. It is for them to rely on and grow in and *never* use as a trick to gain access to children. It is for them to accept the laws of our country and *never* try to play as a 'get out of jail free' card. Grace is a privilege and a responsibility if it is truly the grace of God.

Final thoughts

Thank you for reading this book to the end. The issues we have covered are not easy ones, so I am grateful to you for sticking with it when on occasions you might have felt like putting it down. People have varying amounts of stomach lining when it comes to discussions like this, and what is bearable to one is downright offensive to another. I also recognize that many of you will have been personally affected by child sexual abuse in some form and I particularly commend you for reading a book that will have been desperately painful at times. I am sorry for what you have suffered and the only counsel I can offer you is the assurance that absolutely nothing is impossible for the living Jesus Christ – and that includes the comfort and restoration of hurting people. Indeed, it *especially* includes the comfort and restoration of hurting people. The imagination and creativity that God used to design this amazing planet is the same imagination and creativity he will use to restore anyone who has been damaged by abusers. More than anything else I have written about in this book, I believe in that passionately.

My greatest prayer is that this book will help to protect children. I cannot think of a bigger reward than the fact that someone will learn something from these pages and tighten the protective guard they place around their child.

May God bless you and yours with peace and safety.

Appendix 1:

Useful Contacts

These are the contact details of a few relevant organizations in case you ever need them:

STOP-IT-NOW!
Freephone helpline for abusers seeking help, or the reporting of anyone you are suspicious about.
Phone: 0808 1000 900
Web: www.stopitnow.org.uk

CEOP (Child Exploitation and Online Protection Centre)
For the reporting of any suspicious activity regarding children that you discover on the Internet.
Phone: 0870 000 3344
Web: www.ceop.gov.uk

IWF (Internet Watch Foundation)
For the reporting of any suspicious images or content you see on the Internet.
Phone: 08456 008844
Web: www.iwf.org.uk

ChildLine
Twenty-four-hour helpline for children seeking help regarding any type of distress.
Phone: Freephone 0800 1111
Web: www.childline.org.uk

CCPAS (Churches Child Protection Advisory Service)
Independent Christian charity advising on all areas of child protection.
Phone: 0845 120 4550
Web: www.ccpas.co.uk

Appendix 2:

Church Child Protection System

Here is a summarized version of the child protection system we implemented in our church. Feel free to cherry-pick any sections that you believe would enhance your own system. (You *do* have one, don't you?) No system is perfect and ours was constantly being overhauled, especially as a result of the Jenkins and Mr I cases.

When I stepped down, I imagine it changed again.

Each person asking to work with children was required to complete an *application form* – condensed version follows. It was only when a completed form had been submitted that they were allowed to start working. (It might actually be a good idea to impose a length of time someone needs to be attending the church before they are allowed to even complete a form. After my own experiences regarding Jenkins and Mr I, I have concluded that there is no substitute for just *knowing* someone. I believe children's workers need to be known and accountable within the church for a respectable amount of time before they are in post.) The application form closed with a *voluntary disclosure form* asking individuals to voluntarily disclose any criminal history/concerns relating to children that the *Criminal Record Bureau check* was going to reveal. *Two references* were immediately sought and the Criminal Record Bureau check despatched.

Every six months or so a *training evening* was held at the church and any workers who had not attended one were required to do so as soon as possible. I did visit some people in their homes and deliver the training one-to-one where issues like childcare made attendance at the evening difficult. The training evening itself explained the church policy, defined the different types of child abuse, and covered subjects like how to deal with disclosures of abuse by a child, best practice around children, what to do in the light of suspicions, etc. If any discrepancy was raised at any point in the process, the worker would be required to cease working with children until such time as it was ironed out.

The above procedures all fell under the umbrella of the *church child protection* policy. Many denominations and organizations have their own policy blueprints for churches to adopt. I believe it wiser that you seek their advice when you consider writing your own, rather than me outlining ours. It was tailored to our needs and our staff and would not readily be suitable for re-adoption. But please remember this: while various organizations are available to help you compile your church child protection policy, only you can ensure you have the resolve to enforce it. The most impressive policy is only ever a set of words – it needs people to make it effective. And in the area of child protection it needs very courageous, very committed and very careful people.

(Condensed) APPLICATION FORM FOR PAID OR VOLUNTARY WORK WITH CHILDREN AND YOUNG PEOPLE

This information will be kept confidentially by the church, unless requested by an appropriate authority.

1. Personal Details

We may need to see birth/marriage certificates to check names.

Full name/Maiden, all former names/Date and place of birth/Full address/All daytime and evening telephone numbers, email addresses/Length of time at current address – if less than three years provide all previous addresses with dates.

----

2. Church History

Full account of how and when you became a Christian (i.e. how long have you been a Christian, significant individuals on your journey, the impact on your life, etc.).

Please give details of all previous churches you have attended and dates, name of minister/leader, reason for leaving and any activities undertaken within church.

----

3. Working with Children

Provide thorough details of any qualifications or appropriate training either in a paid or voluntary capacity.

Qualification/training	Date

Provide details of all previous experience of looking after or working with children and/or young people.

Date	Venue	Nature of role/activity

Why do you want to work with children/young people in our church, and what role are you seeking to undertake?

Have you ever had an offer to work with children/young people declined?
❏ YES   ❏NO   (Please tick)
If yes, please give full details.

Do you suffer, or have you suffered, from any illness which may directly affect your work with children or young people?
❏ YES   ❏ NO   (Please tick)
If yes, please give details.

4. Employment History

Please tell us about all your past and current employers in the table below.

Employer's Name & Address	From (Date)	To (Date)	Job Title & Description of Duties	Reason for Leaving

5. References

Please give the names, addresses and telephone numbers and role or relationship of two people who have known you well for at least two years and who would be able to give a personal reference. Please list at least one person from outside the church and do not use family members. In addition we reserve the right to take up character references from any other individuals deemed necessary.

----

6. Declaration

Have you ever been involved in court proceedings concerning a child for whom you have parental responsibility?

❑ YES   ❑ NO   (Please tick)

If yes, please give details and dates.

Has there ever been any cause for concern raised regarding your conduct with children?
❑ YES ❑ NO (Please tick)
If yes, please give details.

To your knowledge, have you ever had any allegation made against you which has been reported to any local authority, e.g. social services, police, education authority.
❑ YES ❑ NO (Please tick)
If yes, we will need to discuss this with you.

All applicants will be required to submit to a criminal records check before the position can be confirmed. This will be an Enhanced Disclosure through the Criminal Records Bureau. As the position is exempted under the Rehabilitation of Offenders Act this check will reveal any details of cautions, reprimands or final warnings, as well as formal convictions. This process is subject to a strict code to ensure confidentiality, fair practice and security of any information disclosed. The CRB Code of Practice and our own procedures are available on request for you to read. It is stressed that a criminal record will not necessarily be a bar to appointment, only if the nature of any matters revealed could be considered to place children or vulnerable adults at risk.

Please would you complete the attached voluntary disclosure form, place it in a sealed envelope and address it to [name of co-ordinator/s] with whom you are welcome to discuss any aspect of this procedure.

Unless required by appropriate authorities, only [name of co-ordinator/s], the minister and [one named elder or deacon etc.] will have access to this information.

I have sent the voluntary disclosure form to [name of co-ordinator/s] in a separate, sealed envelope.

I confirm that the submitted information is correct and complete.

Signed   _____

Date   _____

As a church/organization we undertake to meet the requirements of the Data Protection Act 1998, the Protection of Children Act 1999 and the Criminal Justice and Court Services Act 2000

In addition: The disclosure of an offence may not prohibit employment. Please refer to our Rehabilitation of Offenders Policy. Because of the nature of the work for which you are applying, this position is exempt from the provision of section 4(ii) of the Rehabilitation of Offenders Act 1974 (Exemptions Order 1975), and you are therefore not entitled to withhold information about convictions which for other purposes are 'spent' under the provisions of the Act and, in the event of appointment, any failure to disclose such convictions could result in the withdrawal of approval to work with children and/or young people within the church.

As a church we agree to abide by the Code of Practice on the use of personal data in employee/employer relationships under the Data Protection Act 1998 as well as the expectations of the Criminal Records Bureau/ Scottish Criminal Records Office.

Under the Protection of Children Act 1999 and the Criminal Justice and Court Services Act 2000, it is an offence for any organization to offer employment that involves regular contact with young people under the age of eighteem to anyone who has been convicted of certain specific offences, or included on the PoCA List or DfES List 99.

VOLUNTARY DISCLOSURE FORM

STRICTLY CONFIDENTIAL
All applicants are asked to complete this form (making a 'nil' return if appropriate), returning it in a separate sealed envelope.

To: [Name of co-ordinator/s]
Address: [Address of co-ordinator/s]

Appointment of Children's worker at [name of church] (voluntary)
Voluntary Disclosure
I consent to a criminal records check for the position for which I have applied. I am aware that that details of pending prosecutions, previous convictions, cautions, or bindovers against me will be disclosed along with any other relevant information which may be known to the police, Department of Health or the Department for Education and Skills.

Disclosures
Have you ever been charged with, cautioned or convicted in relation to any criminal offence; or are you at present the subject of criminal investigations/pending prosecution?
❑ YES   ❑ NO   (Please tick)

If yes, please give details including the nature of the offence(s) and dates

_____

Signed _____ Date _____

Last note

Further to this vetting system

- We established that only on-duty Sunday school teachers could take young children to the toilet during Sunday school times, and when they were on-duty the staff wore a badge identifying them as such.
- The main door leading in and out of church had someone present at it before and after the service to ensure that wandering little ones couldn't take it upon themselves to find their own way home while Mum and Dad were distracted!
- Our church child protection policy contained a generalized clause that allowed for the unthinkable to happen – we did not want a policy so specific that something bizarre could come along and technically be outside the remit of all we had outlined. Think laterally at all times! The clause allowed for 'any behaviour or personal history deemed inappropriate by the child protection team' as sufficient to refuse someone permission to work with children.

BROKEN WINGS

*A Breathtaking
Story of Joy,
Hope and Love*

SHEREE OSBORNE

978-1-86024-557-2

secret
scars

One woman's story of
overcoming self-harm

ABIGAIL ROBSON

978-1-85078-721-1